JOURNEY IN DISCIPLESHIP
Living the Spirit-filled Life

© 2010 Godzchild, Inc.

Published by Godzchild Publications
a division of Godzchild, Inc.
22 Halleck St., Newark, NJ 07104
www.godzchildproductions.net

Printed in the United States of America 2010— First Edition
Book Cover designed by Ana Saunders of Es3lla | ARTentional Designs.

All rights reserved. No part of this publication may be reproduced, stored in a retrieval system, or transmitted in any form or by any means – for example, electronic, photocopy, recording – without the prior permission of the publisher. The only exception is brief quotations in printed reviews.

> Library of Congress Cataloging-in-Publications Data
> Journey in Discipleship: Living the Spirit-filled Life/Ray Petty. Includes a study guide and answer key.
>
> ISBN 978-0-9840955-5-1   (pbk.)
> 1. Petty, Ray. 2. Inspirational. 3. Christianity. 4. Devotional.

2010939904

Unless otherwise indicated, Scripture quotations are from the New King James Version of the Bible.

TABLE OF CONTENTS

Introduction | .... *i*

JOURNEY IN DISCIPLESHIP

Chapter 1 |
How Can We Live A Spirit-filled Life?........................ *1*

Chapter 2 |
What is the Mark of a Fruitful Life? *27*

Chapter 3 |
Fulfilling Our Primary Purpose................................ *53*

Chapter 4 |
What's All This Talk about Spiritual Warfare?........ *75*

Chapter 5 |
When It Comes to Spiritual
          Direction – I'm Challenged....................... *101*

Chapter 6 |
Learning to Pray In the Power of the Spirit........... *125*

Chapter 7 |
Jesus – the Ultimate Model
          Of Spirit-filled Living.............................. *151*

Epilogue | *175*

Journey in Discipleship

STUDY GUIDE

Guide for Personal and Group Study | *181*

Lesson 1 |
How Can We Live A Spirit-filled Life?..................... *185*

Lesson 2 |
What is the Mark of a Fruitful Life?..................... *199*

Lesson 3 |
Fulfilling Our Primary Purpose............................. *213*

Lesson 4 |
What's All This Talk about Spiritual Warfare?...... *227*

Lesson 5 |
When It Comes to Spiritual
  Direction – I'm Challenged........................ *243*

Lesson 6 |
Learning to Pray In the Power of the Spirit........... *253*

Lesson 7 |
Jesus – the Ultimate Model
  Of Spirit-filled Living............................. *267*

Notes | *279*

Appendix Answer Key | *283*

Introduction

I am delighted that you have chosen to join me in our journey in discipleship as we purpose to live the Spirit-filled life. This book is written and dedicated to all those who wanted to give up and chose not to. There may have been a dream you had of owning your own business, and time after time it seemed as if the dream was getting further away. There may have been academic goals and aspirations you had and either the timing was wrong, the finances were not there, or job and family responsibilities prevented it from happening. There are so many places in life that we come up against and we wonder if we are up for the task; yet many times when we come to those places, we choose to take the path more traveled, rather than the road less traveled. The decision to keep going when all odds are against you is quite a challenge. When we come to those junctures in our lives, we think to ourselves, "Is it worth it? Do we have what it takes to make it? What if I fail? What will every one think?" Then, we think again, "With God all things are possible" (Matthew 19:26). At that point, God begins to impart a spirit of faith that rises up within us and we declare, "If God is for us, who can be against us?" (Romans 8:31).

One of the things I wanted to do in this book is to weave my own testimony of the transformation Jesus has made and continues to make in my life. You will find several places where wrong choices were made. You will find my own struggle to gain a healthy view of who I am in Christ. But by the grace of God He saved me, filled me with His Holy Spirit, set my feet on a path filled with purpose and destiny; and I am deeply grateful for the extravagant love and unconditional acceptance I have found in Christ. So let's begin our time together by identifying what it means to live a Spirit-filled life.

What does it mean to live a Spirit-filled life? How do we do it? And what difference does it make in our lives? The goal of this book is to address these and other questions that might arise on the journey to discipleship. The Apostle Paul exhorts us not only to live in the Spirit, but also to walk in the Spirit (Galatians 5:25). Again, Paul writes to the church at Corinth, "Now we have

INTRODUCTION

received, not the spirit of the world, but the Spirit who is from God, that we might know the things that have been freely given to us by God" (1 Corinthians 2:12).

So the question arises, *Why does God want us to live a Spirit-filled life?*

First, "God is Spirit and those who worship Him must worship in Spirit and truth" (John 4:24). Second, His Spirit gives us life, "But if the Spirit of Him who raised Jesus from the dead dwells in you, He who raised Christ from the dead will also give life to your mortal bodies through His Spirit who dwells in you" (Romans 8:11). Third, we need the Holy Spirit to assist us in our praying, "Likewise the Spirit also helps in our weaknesses. For we do not know what we should pray for as we ought, but the Spirit Himself makes intercession for us with groanings which cannot be uttered" (Romans 8:26). Fourth, it is the Spirit who produces fruit in our lives, "But the fruit of the Spirit is love..." (Galatians 5:22). Jesus describes it this way, "By this My Father is glorified, that you bear much fruit; so you will be My disciples" (John 15:8). Finally, the Spirit of God releases His gifts through us for the building up of His Church. "Having then gifts differing according to the grace that is given to us, let us use them..." (Romans 12:6). The Spirit of God works through each of us in the uniqueness we bring to the Body of Christ as we share in those Spiritual gifts. This is in no way an exhaustive list, but it gives us a hint about Spirit-filled living.

The next obvious question is: *How can we live the Spirit-filled life?*

Let's bring light to something that can easily be overlooked. Following Jesus' resurrection, He gathered with His disciples and "He breathed on them, and said to them, 'Receive the Holy Spirit'" (John 20:22). After Jesus' ascension, the disciples sought to pray for the promise Jesus had given them, "But you shall receive power when the Holy Spirit has come upon you; and you shall be witnesses to Me in Jerusalem, and in all Judea and Samaria, and to the end of the earth" (Acts 1:8; 1:14; 2:1). Jesus shared with His disciples that He needed to return to the Father so that His Spirit would teach them all things, would lead them into the truth and would always be with them. "And I will pray the Father, and He will give you another Helper, that He may abide with you forever...But the Helper, the Holy Spirit, whom the Father will send in My name, He will teach you all things...However, when He, the Spirit of Truth, has

INTRODUCTION

come, He will guide you into all the truth... (John 14:16, 26, 16:13). How can we live the Spirit-filled life? *It is through our prayerful desire, making ourselves available to the Holy Spirit, and in childlike faith receiving all that the Father desires to give us. My prayer is that the Holy Spirit will impact your life in a way that will transform you.*

I want to express my gratitude to Jim and Linda Noone, Shari Mays and to the greatest encourager and friend Alice, my wife. We went over the chapters so many times. We discussed through endless glasses of lemonade how to make the book meaningful and practical. These times were wonderful and the friendship that grew from our discussions is invaluable.

Blessings in Christ,
Ray Petty, Jr.

Chapter 1
How Can We Live a Spirit-Filled Life?

When I was sixteen, I hit rock bottom. My good friend in high school, Gary, and I had just come back from the movies and went over to his house to get something to eat and everything closed in around me. Up to that point it seemed nothing but failure came my way. I had been held back in the third grade and to make matters worse I had been held back in the fifth grade. I felt like a real loser. My life had no purpose. It was filled with shame, defeat and I was totally out of control. I kept my fears, rejection and anger to myself. I felt as if life had no meaning, so why live. I had no purpose for living. I got up out of the chair and said nothing to Gary as I left the room and went out the door. I was walking down the street toward the highway, to stand in the midst of the oncoming traffic. Gary jumped into his car and caught up with me and asked what I was doing. I told him what I was going to do and he ran toward me, grabbed me and pulled me away from the traffic. Then he forced me back into the car and I wept and wept because I had no idea why God ever created me or brought me into this world. I discovered in a few short weeks that God never gives up on us and loves us when we don't have the love to love ourselves. I would soon discover authentic love, the kind of love that loved me in all my failures, all my mistakes, all my rejections, all my suppressed anger and I found it in the person of Jesus. "Now hope does not disappoint us, because the love of God has been poured into our hearts by the Holy Spirit who was given to us" (Romans 5:5).

    I was sixteen. I had grown up in the Methodist Church and had fond memories of my experience, but one of things we lacked was a real pursuit of the presence and power of God. Therefore, I did not find the church very exciting. Just a few weeks after this experience, our church held a Lay Witness Mission as we invited lay people from other churches to come and share their story about coming to know Jesus and the impact He made in their life. It was during that weekend of witness and small group experience that I encountered the living Christ and had my own personal experience of the Love of God that filled my heart.

Shortly after hosting the Lay Witness Mission, our Pastor, Rev. Bill Warnock, and his wife, Grace, took several of us from the youth group to what was called, Camp Farthest Out (CFO). It was the early days of the Charismatic movement. We heard speakers such as Corrie Ten Boon, Derek Prince, Bob Mumford and Don Basham. For Methodists, this was "far out" because we knew nothing about what they were talking about. Yet, during those days of worship, praise, testimony and teaching, the Lord began stirring my heart for more of Him. I remember the night when I asked Jesus to baptize me in the Holy Spirit. I felt the Holy Spirit infusing me with power like I had put my finger into a light socket. I remember joining the rest of the youth group from our church who had just received the baptism of the Holy Spirit already in the parking lot at 12:30 am, shouting and praising God at the top of our

> I felt the Holy Spirit infusing me with power like I had put my finger into a light socket.

lungs (I think we woke up a lot of people that night). Then, it began to rain and someone said, "This is the confirmation of the rain of God that was sent down into our hearts." While at Camp Fartherest Out, I allowed the Holy Spirit to fill me with Himself and He deposited in me hope, purpose and promise. Then, He put me on a path that would be filled with grace, wonder and surprise. For the first time in my life I felt truly alive. I learned how to study and God put me on a reading course that still continues today. Upon returning from our trip to South Georgia, we began an exciting journey as we sought to walk out our experience with the third person of the Trinity, the Holy Spirit. We were literally traveling in unchartered waters for us spiritually and for our church to love us in the midst of our new zeal and passion for God. We did not know how to walk the Spirit-filled life; the Holy Spirit would be our teacher (John 14:26). God was taking us from "faith to faith" (Romans 1:17), from "grace to grace" (John 1:14) and from "glory to glory" (2 Corinthians 3:17). There was a new desire to pray and to enjoy the fellowship of the Holy Spirit. There was a greater hunger for the word of God and we spent hours soaking in the presence of the Holy Spirit. We not only had a new profound love for God, but a love for others that they might come to experience the love of God in

How Can We Live a Spirit-filled Life?

Jesus Christ. We became bold in our witness about the transformation Jesus was making in our lives as we devoted more of ourselves and our time to Him.

As we returned to our home church we were different people and the church was not quite sure what to do with us, but they loved us and encouraged us in the Lord to stay strong.

My journey had begun as a disciple of Jesus Christ and everything looked different and felt different. I was a new creation in Christ and since then, I have spent the last forty-three years "working out my salvation" (Philippians 2:12).

This was the beginning of living the Spirit-filled life. I began learning to live out of the resources of the Holy Spirit, trusting Him to direct my ways and to fulfill my days with grace, love and the purpose that He placed in my heart.

I invite you to journey with me through the years of learning that I have experienced. I pray that you will keep discovering the wonderful *Comforter* that He is. He knows our weaknesses and brings comfort, encouragement and strength. It was around the age of seventeen that I sensed the call of God to become a pastor. So I set out to attend a two year college, Hiwassee and then transferred to Oral Roberts University and received my M.Div. degree from Asbury Theological Seminary.

The purpose of this book is to draw attention to the work of the Holy Spirit in our daily activity, and to learn how to live the Spirit-filled life. I call it "learning" because there is not a formula that we can memorize and come up with the same results every time. Living the Spirit-filled life is learning to make room for Him every day of our lives by opening our spirit, mind, will and emotions to His impressions, His voice and His promptings.

> Living the Spirit-filled life is learning to make room for Him every day…

In this book we will address seven truths on learning to live the Spirit-filled life: (1) How can we live a Spirit-filled life? (2) What is the mark of a fruitful life? (3) How do we fulfill our spiritual purpose? (4) What's all this talk about spiritual warfare? (5) When it comes to spiritual direction – I'm challenged; (6) Connecting with like-minded people; and (7) Jesus the ultimate model of Spirit-filled living.

There is a study guide for personal and group study that will help to put application to the vital truths and principles for living the Spirit-filled life found at the back of the book entitled *Study Guide.* My prayer is that the Holy Spirit takes possession of us, permeating every area of our lives so that we, like our Model, Jesus, will depend more and more upon the person of the Holy Spirit.

FOUR KEYS TO SPIRITUAL LIVING

SPIRITUAL LIVING KEY #1 |

We discover in the Scriptures at least four keys to spiritual living. The first key to Spirit-filled living is the posture or pose of the heart. A heart that is open to the leading of the Holy Spirit and a heart that responds appropriately to the Lord even in the midst of adversity. We find the church at Thessalonica to be under oppression, tests and trials of all sorts. Yet in the midst of their adversity they responded in such a way that their testimony and witness went out to the surrounding regions about their faith in Jesus Christ (1 Thessalonians 1:6-8).

Spirit-filled living is learning to respond to adversity as we allow the Holy Spirit to fill our hearts with faith and with God's ability to keep us in the midst of trials. Whatever adverse thing you may be facing, God is greater still as you welcome the Holy Spirit into the midst of where you are and make room for Him to move, that He too, will take you from "faith to faith", from "grace to grace" and from "glory to glory." What would it mean for you to open yourself up to the Holy Spirit in the midst of adversity? We are making room for the Holy Spirit to guide us, and to instruct us as we trust the Holy Spirit to show us how to respond to the Spirit's promptings. Let me illustrate what I mean.

In 2 Kings 3:11-18 the kings of Judah, Israel and Edom were going to war against the king of Moab. These kings found themselves in the wilderness of Edom with no water for themselves, nor for their animals and they needed to know that God's hand of blessing and provision was upon them. They also needed to know how they should proceed against the king of Moab.

> We are making room for the Holy Spirit to guide us, and to instruct us as we trust the Holy Spirit…

Sometimes we find ourselves in those hard places that seem to be dry, arid—needing to know God's presence; we need a word of assurance. Jehoshaphat asked a very crucial question: "Is there no prophet of the Lord here, that we may inquire of the Lord by him" (2 Kings 3:11)? In living the Spirit-filled life we depend upon a word from the Lord that encourages us, that confirms we are doing the right things and going in the right direction. Jesus said, "When He, the Spirit of truth, has come, He will guide you into all truth...but whatever He hears He will speak; and He will tell you things to come" (John 16:13).

Jehoshaphat made room for God – to hear what He had to say about the matter. When Jehoshaphat asked that question, he was basically saying, *What does God think about what we are doing? I don't really care what others might be thinking, but I really want to know God's heart on this matter.* Jehoshaphat was guarding himself from what the writer of Proverbs states, "There is a way that seems right to man, but the end is death" (14:12). Making room for God means we make room to hear His voice – for Him to speak to us about a matter. Before he went into battle he wanted to make sure God would be fighting with them. This is living the Spirit-filled life—having the posture of heart intent on being led by the Holy Spirit, getting our direction from Him. God was developing in them a posture of heart as they were being led by the Holy Spirit.

Let's examine this story a bit closer. Jehoshaphat made room by showing them how they needed to respond to the situation they were in. "Thus says the Lord; make this valley full of ditches" (2 Kings 3:16). They made room for God to move as they prepared ditches for Him to fill. They were asking themselves, *How is He going to do it in the desert?* God provided water as He said, "You shall not see wind, nor rain; yet that valley shall be filled with water..." (2 Kings 3:17). Making room for God means I leave room for the supernatural activity of God as He said to them, "Prepare ditches." How many ditches? "Make the valley full of ditches."

God wanted them to get these three truths as they trusted the Spirit's leading:

† When people get desperate enough they will dig ditches so that God can fill them with the water of His Spirit. "For I will pour water on him who is thirsty and floods on the dry ground; I will pour My Spirit..." (Isaiah 44:3).

† Water was beneath their feet; they simply needed to make a place for it to surface, "He turns a wilderness into pools of water, and dry land into water springs" (Psalm 107:35).

† The Lord declared this about where they were "...Yet that valley shall be filled with water, so that you...may drink" (2 Kings 3:17). The word *drink* means to consume, take in; it speaks of openness. God wants to develop in us as we live the Spirit-filled life to have a posture/pose of heart that is open to the Spirit's leading and to the voice of God.

How Can We Live a Spirit-filled Life?

Frank Damazio in his book, *Crossing Rivers Taking Cities,* observes, "Our responsibility is to stop and drink deeply of the rivers of God. 'For our souls shall be like a well watered garden' (Jeremiah 31:12). We must prepare our heart, mind and spirit with expectation and faith to receive. Dig out a place for the Holy Spirit to fill up. Open your hands. Open your spirit. Drink. Absorb. Let the breath of God's Spirit breathe new life in you (John 20:22)." These three kings learned that God's ability to fill up their ditches was not a big deal with Him as they were led by the Holy Spirit to make room for God to move in a miraculous way. "Now it happened in the morning, when the grain offering was offered (worship added), that suddenly water came by way of Edom, and the land was filled with water" (2 Kings 3:20). Jeremiah declares, "Ah, Lord God! Behold, You have made the heavens and the earth by Your great power and outstretched arm. There is nothing too difficult for You" (32:7). Making room for God is having a posture of heart where:

† We invite God into our midst to speak words of grace, peace and assurance.

Frank Damazio, *Crossing Rivers Taking Cities*, Regal, Ventura, Ca., 1999, p. 48.

† We prepare ourselves for Him to fill us with an overflow of His Spirit.

† Let us open ourselves up for God to fill us with Himself – let's start digging!

> The Holy Spirit will enlarge our hearts and give us the capacity to do those things He asks of us.

The Holy Spirit will enlarge our hearts and give us the capacity to do those things He asks of us. What would it take for you to cultivate this kind of posture of heart as you seek to live the Spirit-filled life? We can drink deeply from God's Spirit and be refreshed in His presence. Let us allow the fresh wind of the Holy Spirit to blow upon us and fill us with the capacity to walk in obedience and submission to our heavenly Father.

SPIRITUAL LIVING KEY #2 |

Seeking to live the Spirit-filled life in the fullness of the Holy Spirit, we find a second key; that is the position of the heart. This means to have a heart that is receptive to what the Lord is doing. When we are truly receptive, our heart is positioned in such a way that we welcome the work and ministry of the Holy Spirit into our lives and into the circumstances in which we might find ourselves. I believe this is where God deals with the character of our heart. Before God releases His vision into our hearts or what He is doing or about to do, He deals with our character. If we are not living with integrity, honesty and with godly character, we will not be able to carry His vision. He deals first with the person before He entrusts him with His vision.

I have also discovered living the Spirit-filled life and having the position of my heart to be "clothed with humility" (1 Peter 5:5). There is a sense of humility and brokenness that God brings us to as we allow the Holy Spirit to take possession of our mind, will and emotions. Jesus walked on planet earth with a dependence upon His heavenly Father, for He did nothing that He did not see His Father doing (John 5:19).

Paul's prayer is that we too have the mind of Christ. He came obediently to honor the Father's desire and humbled himself by taking on the heart-position of a servant (Philippians 2:5, 8). This is living the Spirit-filled life: walking in obedience to the Father's pleasure, taking on the position of a heart of a servant, and laying our lives down so that the purposes of God would be fulfilled in us and through us.

The position of the heart speaks of our response to those things around us. It speaks of releasing our faith into those circumstances that seem troubled, unstable and leaning upon the Holy Spirit to navigate us through those adversities in life. The position of the heart speaks of our abiding relationship to our heavenly Father. He wants us to learn this truth, "Apart from Him we can do nothing" (John 15:5). This is where we learn to live out of the resources that God provides. Living out of God's resources will stand the test of time and will establish in us the very character and nature of Christ, "But may the God of all grace, who called us to His eternal glory by Christ Jesus, after you have suffered a while, perfect, establish, strengthen and settle you" (1 Peter 5:10).

> The position of our heart is one of receiving, welcoming the work and ministry of the Holy Spirit.

If the position of our heart is one that demands our own way, demands our rights or has a critical spirit, it affects how we live out the Spirit-filled life. The position of our heart is one of receiving, welcoming the work and ministry of the Holy Spirit. It is learning to say *"Yes"* to God's best, growing as disciples of Jesus Christ and making ourselves available as His servants. Our desire is to be a part of what God is blessing. Spiritual living is a choice we make every day. We choose to live in the fullness of God's blessing and we choose to be refreshed in His presence every day. Is this not our prayer?

> *Lord, Jesus, make us a people wholly dependent upon you. Help us to drink deeply of Your Spirit and cause our spirit to be awakened to your life-giving Spirit. Enlarge our heart's capacity to receive all that You have for us as we seek to live the Spirit-filled life that honors and glorifies Your name. Amen!*

Jack Hayford in His book, *A Passion for Fullness*, defines fullness of the Holy Spirit to mean, "Stretchability as we allow the Holy Spirit to renew the wineskins of our souls, to expand the vision of our understanding, to enlarge our heart for Christ and His redeemed, and to extend our reach to the world." This describes well the position of our heart as we seek to live the Spirit-filled life.

SPIRITUAL LIVING KEY #3 |

The third key we discover about living the Spirit-filled life is described as the purpose of the heart. Job describes the purpose of his heart, "But He knows the way that I take; when He has tested me, I shall come

---

Jack Hayford, *A Passion for Fullness*, Word Publishing, Dallas, Texas, 1990, p. 12.

forth as gold. My foot has held fast to His steps; I have kept His way and not turned aside. I have not departed from the commandment of His lips; I have treasured the words of His mouth more than my necessary food" (Job 23:10-12). The writer of Hebrews captures it well as he describes the prophetic words of the Psalmist speaking of Jesus, "Then I said, 'Behold, I have come in the volume of the book it is written of Me – To do your will, O God'" (Hebrews 10:7). Does this not speak of the purpose of our heart, "To do Your will, O God?" I believe it describes it perfectly. We live with purpose because we are a new creation in Christ. "He made us alive together with Him, having forgiven all your trespasses" (Colossians 2:13).

> Living the Spirit-filled life is a life filled with the purpose of God.

† I can live with purpose when I know that those things that separated me from God and His unconditional love for me, have been wiped out and nailed to the cross (Colossians 2:14).
† I can live with purpose when I know that the river of God's Spirit is flowing through me (John 7:38).

How Can We Live a Spirit-filled Life?

† I can live with purpose as I enjoy the adoption as a son or daughter of God, and walk in my spiritual inheritance (Romans 8:14).

Living the Spirit-filled life is a life filled with the purpose of God. Someone illustrated fulfilling our purpose this way: The coach of the archery team placed a school flag before the students, which consisted of a fish on the flag. The first person said, "I am aiming at the flag." The second person said, "I am aiming at the fish on the flag." Yet another student of the archery team said, "I am aiming at the eye of the fish on the flag." The final member of the team declared, "I am aiming at the pupil on the eye of the fish on the flag."

As we go through life it is easy to lose heart and hard to keep the main thing the main thing. In the midst of a cynical and critical world, it is challenging to keep our focus on the main thing. With all the naysayers of what can and cannot be done, what abilities we have or don't have, it is easy to loose heart and loosen our grip upon God's purpose and plan for our lives. We can become discouraged because it is not quite turning out the way we had planned. The promotion did not come. We have been squeezed into the world's concept of what is success and what is not. Yet our goal is learning to live the Spirit-filled life with all of life's tensions and possibilities. We must give ourselves daily to the Spirit's leading, to His ability to refresh our spirit and to renew our mind.

We find that fulfilling the purpose of God is discovering where we can best serve Him and His church. Learning to live the Spirit-filled life is unwrapping our spiritual gift. God has given gifts to encourage, to build up and to stir one another up to love and good works (Hebrews 10:24). The Apostle Paul exhorted Timothy, "...to stir up the gift of God which is in you through the laying on of my hands" (2 Timothy 1:6). Living the Spirit-filled life is allowing the purpose of God to be fulfilled through the gifts He has given, as He expresses Himself through us.

Spirit-filled living allows us to live in the fullness of God's purpose:

† As we learn to wait upon the Lord. "Wait on the Lord; be of good courage, and He shall strengthen your heart; wait, I say, on the Lord! (Psalm 27:14).

† As the Lord empowers us to do what He calls us to do. "Yet to all who wait upon the Lord shall renew their strength..." (Isaiah 40:31).

How Can We Live a Spirit-filled Life?

† As we are overcome with joy that comes not only as we wait upon the Lord, but also as we are obedient to the Lord. "Behold this is our God; we have waited for Him...we will be glad and rejoice in His salvation" (Isaiah 25:9). We learn to keep the main thing the main thing when we stay the course God has set before us and as we focus on "the Author and Finisher of our faith" (Hebrews 12:2). "Let us not grow weary while doing good, for in due season we shall reap if we do not lose heart" (Galatians 6:9).

SPIRITUAL LIVING KEY #4 |

> ...living the Spirit-filled life is tapping into the promises of God...

We discover that the fourth key to living the Spirit-filled life is tapping into the promises of God. I was attending a daylong workshop on *Preaching to the Next Generation.* The workshop leader began our time together by reading from Deuteronomy 30:11-14, 19-20 (The Message).

"This commandment that I'm commanding you today isn't too much for you, it's not out of your reach. It's not on a high mountain—you don't have to get mountaineers to climb the peak and bring it down to your level and explain it before you can live it. And it's not across the ocean—you don't have to send sailors out to get it, bring it back, and then explain it before you can live it. No. The word is right here and now—as near as the tongue in your mouth, as near as the heart in your chest. Just do it! I call Heaven and Earth to witness against you today: I place before you Life and Death, Blessing and Curse. Choose life so that you and your children will live. And love GOD, your God, listening obediently to him, firmly embracing him. Oh yes, he is life itself, a long life settled on the soil that GOD, your God, promised to give your ancestors, Abraham, Isaac, and Jacob."

    The promises of God are available to all who call upon Him, to all who long to hear His voice, to all who desire to walk in obedience to Him, to all who have failed time and time again, yet they still get back up and pursue God once again. The promises of God are to those described in Proverbs 4:21-22; 25-27 (New Living Translation)."Don't lose sight of them. Let them penetrate deep into your heart, for they bring life to those who find them, and healing to their whole body, look straight ahead, and fix your eyes on what lies before you. Mark out a straight path for your feet; stay on the safe path. Don't get sidetracked; keep your feet from following evil."

    Living the Spirit-filled life is learning to tap into

those promises, allowing God to do His work in us, and walking in the fruitfulness of God. Sometimes it seems as if those promises are a distant memory because they have been so long in coming. Those prophetic words that were spoken over us have become a faint memory of what could have been. Yet to all who wait upon the Lord, who do not become weary in doing good, to all who refuse to faint, but believe the best is yet to come, those promises are still alive and active and are still to be held on to and to be declared over our lives regularly. Knowing that God watches over His word to make sure it comes to pass (Jeremiah 1:12).

Let me illustrate what I mean with the Shunammite woman found in 2 Kings 4:8-37. This is a powerful story of learning to make room for God and getting hold of God's promises as we learn to live the Spirit-filled life. The story begins with the woman desiring to add on to her home in order to make room for the man of God (Elisha) to have a place of quiet and rest. Elisha asked the woman what the desire of her heart was and discovered that she desired to have a child, but was unable to. The promise of the Lord to her was that a year from the time the word was spoken by the prophet, she would have her child. As we learn to live the Spirit-filled life we can proceed through life even if what we have desired has taken a long time to come to fruition. If we have a word of promise to hold on to, we can set our compass and not deviate from the promises of God. Let's detail some of the facts of this story as it unfolds.

† It was a supernatural birth at an appointed time.
† Because she had made room for God, He was going to give her the secret desire of her heart.
† There would be a time of waiting to see the promise fulfilled.

> There is a tendency to lose hope and discouragement sets in...

Job describes it this way, "All the days of my appointed time will I wait, till my change comes" (14:14). We find this same principle at work in Hannah's life as she was given a promise from the Lord about the birth of Samuel found in 1 Samuel 1:20: "So it came to pass...in the course of time that Hannah conceived and bore a son." The time of learning to live the Spirit-filled life and learning to see the promises of God come into fruition between the time when the promise is spoken and the appointed time. During those times, the temptation to loosen our grip on the promises of God is monumental. There is a tendency to lose hope and discouragement sets in. The battle in our mind is to give up and defeat sets in. Yet, we choose, yes, choose this day—life or death—and we choose life! Even if those words of promise are an eternity away. When it seems we are in a valley weeping over the hopes and God's promises are delayed (as described in Psalms 84:5-7), still choose life!

"Blessed is the man whose strength is in You, whose heart is set on pilgrimage. As they pass through the Valley of Baca *(which means weeping)*, they make it a spring; the rain also covers it with pools. They go from strength to strength; each one appears before God in Zion." This is living the Spirit-filled life and trusting God's timetable as He watches over His word to bring it to pass. Our responsibility is not to give up or give in or allow the devil to steal the things that God has placed in our heart.

The promise that God spoke through Elisha to the Shunamimite woman had died. She declared to Elisha, "Why did you bring that promise into our lives only to see it taken away from us?" It would have been better if you had not spoken the promise at all. We all can identify with her broken heart, her dashed dreams and her voice of exasperation. Why? Let's examine a bit closer what she did.

- ✝ She went to where she had made room for God.
- ✝ She laid the prophetic word/promise before God.
- ✝ She pursued God with all her strength.
- ✝ She laid hold of God until He came to the place she had made room for Him.
- ✝ She understood we live by faith and not by sight (2 Corinthians 5:7).

Living the Spirit-filled life waits for resurrection to happen. Elisha came to the place where this woman had made room for God and she discovered that between "strength to strength" and "faith to faith" was the "glory to glory" (2 Corinthians 3:18). This was the place of restored vision, hope and promise. The Shunamimite woman would echo the words of the Psalmist, "Lord, I have loved the habitation of Your house, and the place where Your glory dwells" (26:8). The Lord is the Lord of the resurrection. He resurrects dreams, hopes, promises and fills our destiny, renews our faith and deposits His Spirit into our lives. He wraps His loving arms around us, calls us His sons and daughters and we revel in the fact that we are loved.

Let me conclude our time of examining the different keys of the heart. I don't recall where I found this prayer, but maybe it will become ours together:

How Can We Live a Spirit-filled Life?

I remember the promise You gave me. I still remember it gripped my heart and how it was embedded in my spirit, but God, it seems like it just died. I don't even know where it is anymore, but I'm willing for You to come and lie upon it again, to breathe life into it again. I've made room for You, Lord. There is still a bed reserved only for You in my heart. I've laid my fallen dreams and lifeless promises on Your bed, Lord. Will You come again, as You've done so many, many times before? Come to the room I made for You, and come with purpose. I'm asking You to come – not just for fellowship, not just for a meal, not just to rest – but to raise back to life that which has died.

May God's rich blessings be poured upon you as you live the Spirit-filled life. I invite you to engage yourself and others, and apply the truths and principles found in the study guide section titled, *How Can I Live a Spirit-filled Life?*, in the back of the book (p.185-197).

Chapter 2
WHAT IS THE MARK OF A FRUITFUL LIFE?

There is an image of success, portrayed by the world's system, that we have come to take on ourselves. Everything is measured by that standard and we fall for it hook, line and all. As I struggled to find my identity in the midst of one failure after another, it was hard for me to believe that I really could have a fruitful life. I discovered in my relationship with Jesus Christ, that He will birth in us a fruitful life that honors and glorifies His name. I believe God wants us to do our best and do things with a mindset of excellence. But at times we measure our success by the success of others and we end up frustrated, angry and throw up our hands and say, *What's the use?*

On the other hand, there could be things in our lives that drive us to success but they may not be healthy. We want to be accepted and we want to win approval, but there is a problem if we're only interested in proving a point out of our sense of competiveness and pride.

The Scriptures observe, "Your attitude should be the same that Jesus Christ had. Though he was God, he did not demand and cling to his rights as God. He made himself nothing; He took the humble position of a slave and appeared in human form" (Philippians 2:5-7 NLT). Let me suggest that this is the measure of success that causes us to profit and live a life that honors and glorifies the Lord.

> Your attitude should be the same that Jesus Christ had...

Let's examine what it means to live a fruitful life. What are the characteristics of a fruitful life? Why is it important to live a fruitful life? What is the result of a fruitful life? Matthew's Gospel declares these inviting words of Jesus, "Well done good and faithful servant; you have been faithful over a few things, I will make you ruler of over many things. Enter into the joy of the Lord" (25:23). What we do will not go unnoticed or unappreciated. Our faithfulness to the things that God calls us to—not our achievements, not our accomplishments—but our faithfulness is rewarded, even if it is over a few things, because you never know

What is the Mark of a Fruitful Life?

God's definition of *a few things*. When we have been faithful to what God has called us to do, He promotes and says, "I will make you ruler of many things." Then, we discover there is great joy in doing the things God calls us to do and the very reward itself is *Joy*. I don't labor over the things I cannot change, but I have joy in the fact that what the Lord deems as successful is perfect. I have joy in what He calls me to do and not anyone else, because we all fit together as one in the Body. Each one of us helps to bring completeness to the Body of Christ. I believe the mark of a fruitful life is an enduring life. The *Spirit Filled Life Bible* (NKJV) describes *endurance* as: "The capacity to continue to bear up under difficult circumstances, not with a passive complacency, but with a hopeful fortitude that actively resists weariness and defeat." The characteristic of an enduring life is a fruitful life. Let us ask God to enlarge the capacity of our heart to resist those things that would keep us from living a fruitful life.

Let's look at four types of soil that are found in Mark 4:13-20. We find what makes for a barren life and what makes for a fruitful life. Jesus teaches in Mark 4:13-15, "And He said to them, "Do you not understand

---

Spirit Filled Life Bible, Thomas Nelson Publishers, Nashville, TN, 1991, p. 1884.

this parable? How then will you understand all the parables? The sower sows the word. And these are the ones by the wayside where the word is sown. When they hear, Satan comes immediately and takes away the word that was sown in their hearts."

The first type of soil is the one that is hard, shallow and the seed is unable to penetrate the soil. I would like for us to look at these soils through the word "enduring" and its definition. I will be referring back to the above definition throughout this chapter. First of all, the seed that is sown upon the soil that cannot be penetrated is depicted as passive. The soil has not been ploughed, tilled or prepared to receive the seed that is sown. Therefore, the ability to receive in order to cultivate faithfulness is not there.

The seed that is sown by the wayside is unable to receive the promises of God as stated in Hebrews 10:36, "You have need of endurance, so that after you have done the will of God, you may receive the promise." The Christian faith is not a passive faith but an active one. We are not only called to believe, but also to obey. The soil along the pathway gets beaten down through events, through setbacks, through obstacles that seem insurmountable and any number of things we encounter in life. But the very word that can come to our aid, the

What is the Mark of a Fruitful Life?

very word that can encourage us, the very word that can bring life and liberty is unable to take root, because the soil has lost its ability to endure. The enemy, Satan, comes along in so many different disguises, and steals the very word that would bring life. As a result, we are unable to receive the promises of the Lord. "For the birds of the air come and devour the word that is sown."

It leaves the soil barren, as Frank Damazio's *From Barrenness to Fruitfulness* observes: "Spiritual growth involves a work of God in which the believer cooperates: The principle of human responsibility coupled with God's divine power and promises to produce fruitfulness. "Negligence (leaving soil untilled, unprepared, Added) is a barrenness that is simply the result of a lack of discipline, determination and active faith. We are to make every effort to fulfill God's word over us and in us to become fruitful in (our personal

> Spiritual growth and fruitfulness involve a work of God in which the believer cooperates.

Frank Damazio, *From Barrenness to Fruitfulness*, Regal Books Publications, Ventura, CA, 1998, p. 144.

lives, Added), our ministries and in our churches" (Damazio, 1998).

Let's begin to take responsibility for the soil of our heart, where we have allowed the enemy to steal our destiny, purpose and vision. We must take back the soil the enemy has stolen and begin to till, cultivate and prepare the soil for the seed of the word of God. May this be the mark of the fruitful life.

We find yet another soil described by Jesus in this parable. That is, the rocky soil: "These likewise are the ones sown on stony ground who, when they hear the word, immediately receive it with gladness; and they have no root in themselves, and so endure only for a time. Afterward, when tribulation or persecution arises for the word's sake, immediately they stumble" (Mark 4:16-17 NLT). The word that depicts this soil is resistant. The seed of the word of God is unable to penetrate the stony ground. It insinuates a cluttered life with things that need to be removed in order to make the soil ready for the sowing of the seed. This takes time and a readiness to cooperate with God in the removal of those *stony* things. The opposite of resistant is receptive. It indicates a teachable spirit as described by the Psalmist, "Teach me your ways, O Lord, and lead me in a smooth path" (27:11). It indicates an openness again. He writes,

What is the Mark of a Fruitful Life?

"Open my eyes, that I may see wondrous things from your law" (119:18).

We can allow the *stony* ground to keep tripping us up in our walk with the Lord. In fact, it can become all the excuses we give why we can't grow, why we can't be used of God and the *stony* places become normal; as if they belong there. We become used to them and all the reasons we can't do the things God calls us to do. It is in the midst of those *stony* places that we dig out a place for the Lord to move, to encourage us and to speak to us. Until we speak to the *stones* to be removed and we "....cast [them] into the sea," (Matthew 21:21) they will be the things that distract us, tempt us away from God's presence and discourage us in our pursuit of His presence. We are to take back the ground that the enemy has taken from our hearts.

Bob Sorge in his book, *Unrelenting Prayer* describes the enemy's ploys and tactics to keep the "*stony*" places in our lives. He says, "That's why every device of darkness against your life is focused upon one single issue: To move you from standing before God." Once we begin to dig out the *stony* places, we will have space to stand against the enemy.

Bob Sorge, *Unrelenting Prayer*, Oasis House, Kansas City, Missouri, 2005, p. 21.

The *stony* ground is not unusable soil in which seed can be sown. It simply means it's going to take some time for it to get ready. There are areas in our lives where we give up on something, or we think we will never get a breakthrough from that addiction that has plagued us all our lives. Or, perhaps finances seems as if they will never get better. These *stony* places can be healed and managed as we begin to remove those obstacles and make room for God to speak to us about those areas in our lives. We must be courageous enough to address the *stony* places so that when we are attacked on every side and the Adversary comes, we can declare, "Thus far and no more! Here is where I take my stand! I refuse to do those things that have held me captive all my life or revert to the way I have always handled adversity." Those things steal our joy, rob us of our peace and take us off course from God's purpose and destiny for our lives.

> We must be courageous enough to address the "stony" places...

I remember in my early teens, my Dad decided to reseed our entire yard. There was truckload after truck load filled with dirt that was dumped all around our home. When the last truck drove away, I was the happiest guy in the neighborhood. Then came the hard work of spreading the dirt to cover the yard with dirt that had more rocks and debris in it than I could ever imagine. In order for the yard to come out looking nice, we had to get all the rocks out and make it a place where seed could be sown, grow up and become a beautiful lawn. The Apostle Paul explains what happens as we allow God to do some deep work in our lives, "But we all, with unveiled face, beholding as in a mirror the glory of the Lord, are being transformed into the same image from glory to glory, just as by the Spirit of the Lord" (2 Corinthians 3:18). We are God's workmanship created in Christ Jesus for good works (Ephesians 2:10). Just because we have some rocks in the way, it doesn't mean they can't be removed; it just means we are a work in progress and we need to receive God's picture of who we are in Him and what He desires to do in our lives.

    The third type of soil is covered with thorns. Jesus describes the soil this way, "Now these are the ones sown among thorns; they are the ones who hear the word, and the cares of this world, the deceitfulness of riches, and the desire for other things enter in, choke the word, and it becomes unfruitful" (Mark 4:18-19). This describes a life full of distractions, misguided ambitions and questionable values. The word that best describes this soil is 'defeated.' Let me explain, not defeated in the sense that a person is hopeless. Not defeated in the sense that they have lost something (though they have), but defeated in the sense that they are living life at the lowest common denominator. They value stuff, instead of valuing who they are and whose image they bear. They are more attracted to things and the accumulation of things, than in gaining the heart of a servant. Jesus makes this observation in Matthew 16:25-27, "If you try to hang on to your life, you will lose it. But if you give up your life for my sake, you will save it. And what do you benefit if you gain the whole world but lose your own soul? Is anything worth more than your soul?"

> "If you try to hang on to your life, you will lose it."

    Sometimes the undergrowth can be unforgiveness, and unforgiveness can bring barrenness to our lives. We were traveling with another family from our church to a conference and as we were passing through Cincinnati, Ohio the husband turned to me and asked, "How long will it take me to forgive those who hurt us?" Jim and his wife had been hurt by the leadership of the church and Jim was carrying the wounds that he and his wife had experienced. Jim was having a very difficult time moving

What is the Mark of a Fruitful Life?

forward in his relationship with Christ and in his relationship with others. He wondered could he ever trust leadership again. The Holy Spirit helped me to answer Jim's question and my response was, "Jim, whenever you decide to. That is how long it will take. It can be a moment or a lifetime. The choice is yours."

The undergrowth of unforgiveness, revenge and anger will abort any seed that God might sow into your life. God wants us to experience His freedom and not to walk in the bondage of our sin. The key is that we walk in love and give it away. Forgiveness is a choice, to receive Christ's forgiveness and to forgive ourselves. This is preparing the soil of our heart for the good word of God to be sown into our lives and to grow up and bear fruit. We must not leave one thing in our lives for the enemy to come and hang his garbage on.

The story is told of a mission team who, while visiting Haiti, heard a Haitian pastor illustrate total commitment to his congregation.

A certain man wanted to sell his house for $2,000. Another man wanted very badly to buy it, but because he was poor, he couldn't afford the full price. After much bargaining, the owner agreed to sell the house for half the original price with just one stipulation: he would retain ownership of one *small nail protruding from just over the door. After several years, the original owner wanted the house back, but the new owner was unwilling to sell. So the first owner went out, found the carcass of a dead dog, and hung it from the single nail he still owned. Soon the house became unlivable, and the family was forced to sell the house to the owner of the nail. The Haitian pastor's conclusion: If we leave the Devil with even one small peg in our life, he will return to hang his rotting garbage on it, making it unfit for Christ's habitation.*

There is an interesting story found in 2 Kings 6:13-18, "And it was told him, saying, 'Surely [Elisha] is in Dothan.' Therefore he sent horses and chariots and a great army there, and they came by night and surrounded the city. And when the servant of the man of God arose early and went out, there was an army, surrounding the city with horses and chariots. And his servant said to him, 'Alas, my master! What shall we do?' So he answered, 'Do not fear, for those who are with us are more than those who are with them.' And Elisha prayed, and said, 'LORD, I pray, open his eyes that he may see.' Then the LORD opened the eyes of the young man, and he saw. And behold, the mountain was full of horses and chariots of fire all around Elisha. So when the Syrians came down to him, Elisha prayed to the LORD, and said, 'Strike this people, I pray, with blindness.' And He struck them with blindness according to the word of Elisha. The King of Syria had surrounded Elisha and his young servant. The servant rose early and discovered they were surrounded by a host of chariots and horses."

The *first peg* that had to be removed from the spiritual house of his young servant was the undergrowth of fear. "Do not fear, for those who are with us are more than those who are with them" (2 Kings 6:15b-16). John in his Epistle writes, "There is no fear in love, but perfect love casts out fear, because fear involves torment" (1 John 4:18). The enemy that had come against Elisha and his servant sought to strike fear in their hearts and minds. Paul writes, "For God has not given us a spirit of fear, but of power and of love and of a sound mind" (2 Timothy 1:7). Fear has a way of blinding us from the truth, robbing us of our peace and paralyzing us in our faith. Francis Frangipane in an Elijah List posting entitled, *Expect to See God's*

> Fear has a way of blinding us from the truth…and paralyzing us in our faith.

Glory! Light Shines in the Darkness states, "Never mistake temporary darkness for permanent blindness, for today's training is the very process that opens us to see God's glory." Ultimately, we will discover the truth of what Isaiah wrote, that "...the whole earth is full of [God's] glory" (Isaiah 6:3). Lord, open our eyes!

The *second peg* that had to be removed from the spiritual house of his young servant was the undergrowth of unbelief. Paul describes his own eye opening experience with Christ and God's call upon his life, "To open their eyes, in order to turn them from darkness to light, and from the power of Satan to God, that they may receive forgiveness of sins and an inheritance among those who are set apart by faith in Me" (Acts 26:18).

We must deal with any pegs that we have allowed the enemy to have in our lives:

† It could be that we do not realize we have a peg in our life, and the enemy has an opportunity to hang his stuff on it.

† It could be that it does not bother us that the enemy hangs his stuff on the peg of our life, because we have become accustomed to it being there.

Frangipane, Francis. *Expect to See God's Glory: Light Shines in the Darkness.* 4 May 2010. 1 Oct. 2010
http://www.elijahlist.com/words/display_word/8728.

What is the Mark of a Fruitful Life?

† It could be that we do not want the peg removed because it may require our giving more of ourselves to Christ than we are willing to give.

Let me illustrate with this graphic:

DEALING WITH THE THORNS AND THE UNDERGROWTH

The servant said, "Alas, my master! What shall we do?" (2 Kings 6:15b)

"Now the Lord is the Spirit, and where the Spirit of the Lord is, there is liberty" (2 Corinthians 3:17).

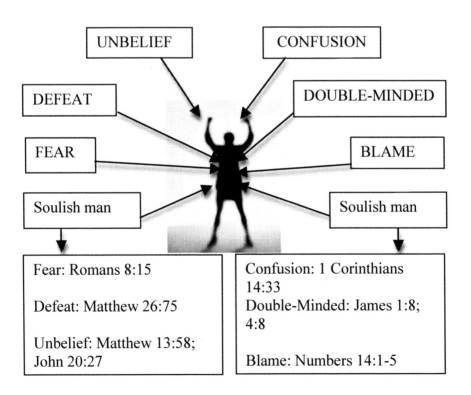

"We must determine to grow spiritually. Such growth is painful because one undergoes stretching, molding, and refining by the Holy Spirit. Spiritual people deal ruthlessly with any thoughts, behaviors, or habit patterns that are destructive and are contrary to the Spirit of God."

Dealing with the thorns and the undergrowth to make it receptive to the word of God is what brings transformation, healing and release.

Fear: "For you did not receive the spirit of bondage again to fear, but you received the Spirit of adoption by whom we cry out, "Abba, Father" (Romans 8:15).

Defeat: And Peter remembered the word of Jesus who had said to him, "Before the rooster crows, you will deny Me three times." So he went out and wept bitterly" (Matthew 26:75).

Unbelief: "Now He did not do many mighty works there because of their unbelief" (Matthew 13:58). Then He said to Thomas, "Reach your finger here, and look at My hands; and reach your hand here, and put it into My side. Do not be unbelieving, but believing" (John 20:27).

Spirit-Filled Life Study Bible, Thomas Nelson Publishers, Nashville, TN, 1991.

What is the Mark of a Fruitful Life?

Confusion: "For God is not the author of confusion but of peace, as in all the churches of the saints" (1 Corinthians 14:33).

Double-minded: "He is a double-minded man, unstable in all his ways. Draw near to God and He will draw near to you. Cleanse your hands, you sinners; and purify your hearts, you double-minded" (James 1:8, 4:8).

Blame: So all the congregation lifted up their voices and cried, and the people wept that night. And all the children of Israel complained against Moses and Aaron, and the whole congregation said to them, "If only we had died in the land of Egypt! Or if only we had died in this wilderness! Why has the LORD brought us to this land to fall by the sword, that our wives and children should become victims? Would it not be better for us to return to Egypt?" So they said to one another, "Let us select a leader and return to Egypt." Then Moses and Aaron fell on their faces before all the assembly of the congregation of the children of Israel" (Numbers 14:1-5).

> *Lord, I confess my fears of (name those fears) and ask Your forgiveness. Lord, I renounce the fear of (name each one) and close the door of my heart, mind, will and emotions to these fears and declare these fears no longer have power over my life. Lord, I receive Your forgiveness and Your freedom from these fears. "Whom the Son sets free is free indeed" (John 8:36).*

List the different kinds of fears people might have.

_____

_____

_____

_____

† What is your greatest fear?
† What are the things that provoke fear in your heart?
† What keeps you from walking in God's peace?

Let's turn to the last soil, *enduring*. Jesus addresses fruitfulness, "But these are the ones sown on good ground, those who hear the word, accept it, and bear fruit: some thirtyfold, some sixty, and some a hundred" (Mark 4:20). Enduring is: *The capacity to continue to bear up under difficult circumstances, not with a passive complacency, but with a hopeful fortitude that actively resists weariness and defeat.*

This is keeping our focus on Christ while we journey as disciples of Jesus Christ, "Let us run with endurance the race that is set before us" (Hebrews 12:1).

What is the Mark of a Fruitful Life?

For the very mark of a disciple of Jesus is "That we bear much fruit; so you will be My disciples...And that your fruit should remain" (John 15:8, 16).

THE FIVE SPIRITUAL CHARACTERISTICS TO LIVING A FRUITFUL LIFE
SPIRITUAL CHARACTERISTIC #1 |

First of all, that we are connected to Christ in a vital relationship to Him called *abiding*, "Yes, I am the vine; you are the branches. Those who remain in Me, and I in them, will produce much fruit. For apart from Me you can do nothing" (John 15:5). To abide means to have a vital, growing and maturing walk with Jesus Christ. He really wants us to realize that apart from Him we can do absolutely nothing that will bear fruit over the long haul, through the adversity, through the ups and downs in life.

Frank Damazio observes, "The power of abiding in Christ, abiding in His presence, this is the principle of preservation. This is the secret to a long life of fruitfulness: presenting ourselves constantly before His presence because in ourselves we are dry and barren. Our reliance is upon God for our fruitfulness." Jesus wants us to get this truth, apart from Him we can do nothing at all!

Frank Damazio, *From Barrenness to Fruitfulness*, Regal Books Publications, Venture, CA, 1998, p. 172.

SPIRITUAL CHARACTERISTIC #2 |

The second spiritual characteristic to living a fruitful life is adding qualities of Christ into our lives. "But also for this very reason, giving all diligence, add to your faith virtue, to virtue knowledge, to knowledge self-control, to self-control perseverance, to perseverance godliness, to godliness brotherly kindness, and to brotherly kindness love. For if these things are yours and abound, you will be neither barren nor unfruitful in the knowledge of our Lord Jesus Christ" (2 Peter 1:5-8).

> God wants to add to our lives those qualities that demonstrate Christ-likeness...

God wants to add to our lives those qualities that demonstrate Christ-likeness and we must be intentional in our pursuit of those godly qualities as George Barna makes note, "Becoming a complete and competent follower of Jesus Christ. It is about intentional training of people who voluntarily submit to the Lordship of Christ and who want to become imitators of Him in every thought, word and deed."

George Barna, *Growing True Disciples*, Water Brook Press, Colorado Springs, CO, 2001, p. 17.

What is the Mark of a Fruitful Life?

We lay aside every weight, and sin that so easily ensnares us and we run with endurance the race that is set before us with diligence. Peter states clearly when we are diligent in adding to our life through our abiding relationship to Jesus Christ the promise is, "You will be neither barren nor unfruitful in growing, in knowing and in experiencing God."

SPIRITUAL CHARACTERISTIC #3 |

The third spiritual characteristic to living a fruitful life is accepting Christ's discipline into our lives. "Now no [disciplining] seems to be joyful for the present, but painful; nevertheless, afterward it yields the peaceable fruit of righteousness to those who have been trained by it" (Hebrews 12:11). God is interested in the end product of us living a fruitful life. Now it may take different paths for each one of us, because we are uniquely made, designed and fashioned by God, our Creator and He knows what it takes for "Christ to be formed in us" (Galatians 4:19). If we go kicking and screaming through the adversity, is not the process lengthened? Though God did not create those things, He uses them to form Christ in us as we remain in our abiding relationship to Him.

SPIRITUAL CHARACTERISTIC #4 |

The fourth spiritual characteristic to living a fruitful life is opening ourselves to Christ's authority in our lives. "That you may walk worthy of the Lord, fully pleasing Him, being fruitful in every good work and increasing in the knowledge of God..." (Colossians 1:10).

Living the Spirit-filled life is to humble yourself under the mighty hand of God (1 Peter 5:6). It means submitting yourself to His Lordship in your life. "Being fruitful in every good work" begins with a humble and contrite heart.

John Bevere observes, "It is not just outward obedience that God requires, but a broken and contrite heart, one that thirsts and hungers for the will of God." David describes it this way, "For you do not desire sacrifice, or else I would give it...the sacrifices of God are a broken spirit, a broken and contrite heart – These, O God, You will not despise" (Psalm 51:16-17). The truth is, if we have trouble with delegated authority, those whom God has placed over our lives for our good and for His glory, we will constantly have trouble with God's authority in our lives.

John Bevere, *Under Cover*, Thomas Nelson Publishing, Nashville, TN, 2001, p. 20.

What is the Mark of a Fruitful Life?

Again, Bevere observes how someone might say, "I submit to God, but not to man, unless I agree with him." This is where our upbringing and incorrect church thinking can hinder us. We cannot separate our submission to God's inherent authority from our submission to His delegated authority."

All authority originates from Him! We find in Romans 13:1-2 "Let every soul be subject to the governing authorities. For there is no authority except from God, and the authorities that exist are appointed by God. Therefore whoever resists the authority resists the ordinance of God, and those who resist will bring judgment on themselves." So we see there is a direct correlation between our submitting to Christ's Lordship in our lives and our obeying the spiritual authority God has placed us under.

The last spiritual characteristic to living a fruitful life is to abound in laboring with Christ. "So, my dear brothers and sisters, be strong and unmovable. Always work enthusiastically for the Lord, for you know that nothing you do for the Lord is ever useless" (1 Corinthians 15:58 New Living Translation). The New King James Version translates, "Therefore, my beloved brethren, be steadfast, immovable, always abounding in the work of the Lord, knowing that your labor is not in vain in the Lord."

The word *abounding* means excess, excel, the generosity of God's grace. We are called to do God's work and ministry with excellence. It is God's grace working in you and through you that enables, equips and empowers you to fulfill that calling, ministry or assignment.

The Christian faith is not a passive faith but an active one. We are not only called to believe, but also to obey! True faith produces loving obedience. Holy desperation for God's presence creates an enduring faith that results in a fruitful life.

The question we began with was, *How can we live a fruitful life?* Fruitfulness comes out of our abiding relationship to Jesus Christ. It comes out of a life that is willing to personally deal with the soil of our heart that makes it hard to receive God's blessings, His work and plan. It is making those tough decisions and allowing God to do some deep plowing in our heart to remove those things that trip us up. It is when we come to the reality that apart from Christ, what we seek to do will never have the eternal affect upon our lives; that is the point that God wants us to get at. Jesus said, "You did not choose Me, but I chose you and appointed you that you should go and bear fruit, and that your fruit should

---

Spirit-Filled Life Study Bible, Thomas Nelson Publishers, Nashville, TN, 1991, p. 1455.

remain, that whatever you ask the Father in My name He may give you" (John 15:16).

May God's rich blessings be poured upon you as you live a fruitful life in Christ Jesus. I invite you to engage yourself and others, and apply the truths and principles found in the study guide section titled, *How Can I Live a Fruitful Life?*, found in the back of the book (p.199-212).

Chapter 3
FULFILLING OUR PRIMARY PURPOSE

Fulfilling our primary purpose cannot exist outside of a vital growing relationship to Jesus Christ. The Apostle Paul exhorts the men of Athens on Mars Hill with this statement about Jesus Christ, "For in Him we live and move and exist..." (Acts 17:28 NLT). Following our encounter with the Lord, our youth group would gather regularly after school to either go to the church to pray, or we would go to our pastor's home where Grace, our pastor's wife, would lead us in a time of devotion and prayer. God was dealing deeply in our lives as we sought to know Him more and more. We were hungry for God. I sensed God's call to ministry, but was not fully convinced, so I began visiting the local nursing homes and hospitals. I stopped by rooms and visited with the folks and had prayer with them. I remember stopping by one person's room, and about half way through our conversation she said to me, "Are you going into the ministry?" I replied that I was praying about that and was not sure. A few days passed and what that lady spoke to me intrigued me so much, I thought I would go back and visit with her again to inquire why she asked me that question. I went back to the floor and to the room where she had been and she was not there. I went to the nurses station and inquired about the lady and I told them how long she had been in the hospital and they said, "They had never had a patient that long." So, I went to every floor in the hospital and to each of the nurse stations and no one knew of her existence. I think I encountered what the writer of Hebrews describes as an "angels without realizing it" (13:2). The Lord knew all about my background and all the struggles I had encountered. He even knew that I needed to know with certainty His plan, purpose and destiny He had for me and would be my "Helper" as Jesus said, "And I will pray the Father, and He will give you another Helper, that He may abide with you forever" (John 14:16). Jesus knew full well His

> The Lord knew all about my background and all the struggles I had encountered...

purpose, "Now My soul is troubled, and what shall I say? 'Father, save Me from this hour?' But for this purpose I came to this hour" (John 12:27). Jesus said, "For the Son of Man has come to seek and to save that which was lost" (Luke 19:10). John in his Epistle states yet another reason for Jesus' coming, "He who sins is of the devil, for the devil has sinned from the beginning. For this purpose the Son of God was manifested, that He might destroy the works of the devil" (1 John 3:8). Our heavenly Father wants us to know and to walk in His purpose, plan and destiny which He has for each of His children. He does not want His children to go groping through life unfulfilled, frustrated and disappointed; but fulfilled, joyful and fruitful. We may not have angelic visitations or claps of thunder or any extravagant experience, but just the "Still small voice" (1 Kings 19:12) of the Spirit speaking to us about fulfilling our primary purpose is sometimes more than enough. You may ask, *What is our primary purpose?*

Journey in Discipleship

I would use this acronym of F.O.C.U.S. to describe our primary purpose:

F ulfilling our primary purpose is connecting people to Jesus.

O bedient to the Great Commission and the Great Commandment.

C ommitted to the values, vision and mission of the local church.

U nity of the Body of Christ, where God has commanded blessings.

S piritual growth and maturity.

This leads us to asking several questions:

† What are we doing to connect people to Jesus and His church? Mel Lawrenz states, "Getting people personally engaged with God is where the ministry of the church begins."

† What are we doing to fulfill the Great Commission and the Great Commandment?

† What are we doing to create a healthy church, helping people to find their place of ministry and service and to give expression to their gifts and passion?

Mel Lawrenz, *Whole Church: Leading from Fragmentation to Engagement*, Jossey-Bass, San Francisco, CA, 2009, p. 30.

Fulfilling Our Primary Purpose

† What are we doing to enhance the unity of the church?

† What are we doing to cultivate spiritual growth and maturity?

If our primary purpose in life is wrapped up in what we do for a living—that is, the accumulation of things we have gathered, accomplishment of things we have done or the acquisition of the things we have gained—then we will be sorely disappointed when our journey in this life is completed.

> We can find purpose when we are displaying a life that honors and glorifies God...

Let me suggest that our primary purpose is threefold. First, it is devoting ourselves to having a servant's heart. If Jesus came serving and giving, then those who follow Him will do likewise, "If anyone serves Me, let him follow Me; and where I am, there My servant will be also..." (John 12:26). Second, it is devoting our life to be fully committed to the Lordship of Jesus in our life. The writer of Proverbs notes, "Trust in the Lord with all your heart, and lean not on your own understanding; in all your ways acknowledge Him, and he shall direct your paths" (3:5-6). Third, is demonstrating a sacrificial life, "I beseech you therefore, brethren, by the mercies of God that you present your bodies a living sacrifice..." (Romans 12:1). We can find purpose when we are displaying a life that honors and glorifies God, in our serving, giving and worship to the Lord of all the earth.

    I was learning to walk out what the Holy Spirit was teaching me, because He is our *Teacher,* for He will teach us all things, "But the Helper, the Holy Spirit, whom the Father will send in My name, He will teach you all things..." (John 14:26). I hid in my heart those words spoken in that hospital room. I hid in my heart the opportunities to share and preach at neighboring churches and hear of people's response to the love of Christ. I hid in my heart the closing night at camp when I shared my testimony of the love of Christ and watched and heard young people giving their lives to Him. I hid in my heart while sharing at a Lay Witness Mission in Bluefield, VA following the football game as we gathered in the living room of a member of the Methodist church and began sharing Christ and His love, and hearing young people again moved by the Holy Spirit giving their lives to Christ. I struggled for years to believe that God could use me in His service and wanted to give up again and again. This sense of inadequacy, failure and embarrassment filled my life. It was the encouragement of my wife, however, to keep moving forward and to complete the course that God had placed before us. God would continue to put people in my life that He would use to strengthen my walk with Christ, growing as a disciple of Jesus Christ and His equipping for service and ministry.

Don't let the enemy steal your victory, your destiny or your identity in Christ Jesus. He made you, created you and filled your heart with purpose. Silence his voice by rejecting his lies, his deception; his ploy and plots to keep you in bondage, to take you off course from your destiny and keep you from fulfilling your primary purpose. "If God be for you (and He is added)...Who shall separate us from the love of Christ? Shall tribulation, or distress, or persecution, or famine, or nakedness, or peril, or sword? Yet in all these things we are more than conquerors through Him who loved us. For I am persuaded that neither death nor life, nor angels nor principalities nor powers, nor things present nor things to come, nor height nor depth, nor any other created thing, shall be able to separate us from the love of God which is in Christ Jesus our Lord" (Romans 8:31, 35. 37-39).

In fulfilling our primary purpose there are several questions we must entertain: First, why am I here; how is my life going to have meaning? Where will I find my sense of significance? Second, where am I going? Last, who am I? When we are able to answer these questions with assurance, we are on the way to fulfilling our primary purpose.

I remember struggling with my sense of identity, because of the many obstacles I had to overcome to meet college entrance requirements, completing my courses with a solid GPA because it was necessary to get into graduate school (seminary). Yet I discovered God's grace and abilities He imparts to complete the thing He calls us to do. Someone said, *He not only calls us, but He also equips us.* God puts us on a course where we at times have to press through and not give into the temptation to stop short of God's call and destiny on our life. The temptation to loosen our grip and to settle for less than God's best is always before us. The temptation to settle for good over the best is a struggle we all face. I had to learn endurance, the ability to stick with it until the task

> The temptation to settle for good over the best is a struggle we all face.

Fulfilling Our Primary Purpose

is completed. The temptation to run is always the way of escape, but I found out that the things we run from will always come up again and again until we learn to face it, deal with it and thank God for the character of Christ that is being formed in us.

Let us examine those questions in light of Anna, a prophetess, the daughter of Phanuel (Luke 2:36-38). We find that Anna's husband died while she was young and she remained a widow for eighty-four years, "Who did not depart from the temple, but served God with fasting and prayers, night and day" (Luke 2:37). How did she answer those looming questions: Where will I find my significance? Where am I going? Who am I? There is not one of us to some degree or another who hasn't wrestled with these questions. Jesus said, "When the Spirit of Truth comes, He would lead us into all the truth" (John 16:13). The Holy Spirit will tell us the truth about our significance. He will tell us the truth of who we are in Christ Jesus. He will tell us the truth about where we are going, not just a destination, but a destiny.

Michael Slaughter observes, "Only by learning to listen to the Holy Spirit can you fulfill your deepest

---

Michael Slaughter, *Real Followers*, Abingdon Press, Nashville, TN, 1998, p. 43.

driving thirst to have a relationship with the living God and to fulfill your created purpose."

Anna discovered her significance not by trying to create something or make something happen. Rather it was in the solitude of waiting, watching with anticipation of what the Lord would do as she quieted herself before the Lord. The Psalmist observes, "Be still, and know that I am God..." (46:10). In those long hours, days, months and years as Anna quieted her heart before the Lord, He was, "...putting His word in her mouth and had hidden her safely in His hand" (Isaiah 51:16). This enabled her to "...talk about Jesus to everyone who had been waiting for the promised King to come and deliver Jerusalem" (Luke 2:38).

> [Anna]'s significance was simply in being loved by God, enjoying His presence every day...

Anna learned to pray through the trials, tests and adversity. "...she never left the temple...worshiping God...with prayer" (Luke 2:37). Do you think she got tired of waiting? Do you think she had a discouraging thought to run through her mind? Do you think others ridiculed her or made fun of her, as she waited to see the coming Lord? Do you think she ever got weary of staying

Fulfilling Our Primary Purpose

in the same spot for over 60 years? Her significance was not dependent upon what others were thinking or saying. Her significance was simply in being loved by God, enjoying His presence every day and being the vehicle through whom God would encourage the parents of Jesus, the Son of God. Out of that deep dependence upon God and waiting upon the revelation of the Son of God, she was able to speak to others about Him, because she learned to cultivate a listening ear to hear what God was saying. Our significance is identified, cultivated and developed in our time of waiting. Anna learned this secret, "Don't get tired of doing what is good. Don't get discouraged and give up, for we will reap a harvest of blessing at the appropriate time" (Galatians 6:9). Anna's life is best described in Psalm 26:8 "Lord, I have loved the habitation of your house and the place where your glory dwells." Anna's challenge was not to agonize over what she had missed, but to discover whom she would look upon and her eyes would behold, the Son of God.

Let's examine more closely these pivotal questions: Why are we here? Where will we find our sense of significance? There is within each of us a desire to know that we have something of value to contribute. We want

---

Mel Lawrenz, *Whole Church: Leading from Fragmentation to Engagement*, Jossey-Bass, San Francisco, CA, 2009, p. 53.

our ideas, hopes and dreams to be heard, acknowledged and appreciated. Yet, at times those contributions get sidetracked, derailed or they get placed on the back burner only to be forgotten about and never again retrieved.

Mel Lawrenz describes the heart this way, "The heart is the inner sanctum. It is the Holy of Holies. It is where people engage with God." There is something in the heart of mankind that is uniquely placed there by God. Some have described it as a *void* in the heart of man that only God can fill. God wants us to know that outside of a vital relationship with His Son, Jesus Christ, our significance will not truly come to fruition or reach its full potential. God designed it to be that way.

God created us for community where we find our place of significance and service in community life. While attending Oral Roberts University, my wife and I had our first experience with community. The chaplain at ORU was Rev. Bob Stamps and he brought together some of the married couples for support, prayer, Bible study and encouragement. We met each Thursday evening for approximately two hours for fellowship, worship, study of the word and communion. We learned not only what it meant to engage ourselves with God, but we also learned what it meant to be engaged with others, building life-long relationships. It was one of the most impactful experiences we had. It became a model for us as we sought to build small groups in the churches we served. We discovered our place of significance in the place of fellowship with other like-minded believers. We understood what the early church did as described in Acts 2:42 "And they continued steadfastly in the Apostles' doctrine and fellowship, in the breaking of bread, and in prayers."

> Anna discovered her significance in the quiet place, alone with God.

Michael Slaughter describes community, "Radical discipleship is formed in authentic community. Life transformation occurs most readily in biblical community. Discipleship happens as people come together and live in Koinonia of the Spirit." Anna discovered her significance in the quiet place, alone with God. She carefully listened to His voice, and no one was watching and meditating on the wonderful things He was depositing in her heart that she would soon speak to

---

Michael Slaughter, *Unlearning Church*, Group Publishing, Loveland, CO, 2002, p. 141.

others about. "And coming in that instant she gave thanks to the Lord, and spoke of Him to all those who looked for redemption in Jerusalem" (Luke 2:38). She also discovered her significance in the community who gathered around this new born babe, Jesus and began to speak of all the things God had spoken to her about this Jesus. Hearing God's voice is not a private matter. It is for the betterment, the equipping and the encouraging of the Body of Christ. What we hear must become public and it becomes good news. Anna became one of the first evangelists as she bore witness to the redemption in Jerusalem; she was a "Burning bush." Though Joseph and Mary did not know the full implication of what Anna was sharing, they understood that God was about to do something new and they were going to be a part of it.

We discover another question that Anna had to answer: Where am I going? Since she experienced the death of her husband, she now lived on her own, in her own private world. She made some choices about how she would spend her time and finally chose the best place where that could happen—in the temple doing those things that would give birth to the Son of God – prayer and intercession. I know one of the questions that consumed my thinking was; where am I going? That was the frustrating element of living outside a vital

Fulfilling Our Primary Purpose

relationship to Jesus Christ. I had no idea where I was going. I was still trying to figure out how God could have made such a mistake in creating me and bringing me into this world with all the challenges, setbacks and discouraging words I would encounter. I remember the words that were etched on my mind when my fifth grade teacher said to me, "By the time you are sixteen, you will either be behind bars or six foot under." I had only one way to go and that was up. In Junior High, I remember walking into the principal's office and telling him that I wanted to take the track that would prepare me for college. Up until that time with all the repeating of grades that I encountered, the school system already knew how far I could or would go. The system had already identified me as a slow learner and therefore, placed me in classes with those who were not interested in being there. They seemed to always be in trouble and I too was always at the wrong place at the wrong time. God was beginning to work in my life just to have the courage to *stand up for myself and to challenge the system.* In my heart of hearts I knew there was more but it was so illusive. I could never get a hold of it. I discovered that where I am going is not just a destination point, but a destiny that I have in Christ. It is not a place of arrival, but a quality of life that becomes the gospel, a life surrendered to the Lordship of Jesus Christ. I believe Anna modeled this quality of life in her pursuit of living forty-seven years in the presence of God. Paul's letter to Titus describes well that quality of life, "We should live soberly, righteously, and godly in this present age, looking for the blessed hope and glorious appearing of our great Savior Jesus Christ" (2:12-13). The place where Anna would discover is the "secret place" described by the Psalmist, "He who dwells in the secret place of the Most High shall abide under the shadow of the Almighty" (91:1).

> ...live soberly means "To act in a responsible manner, sensibly, prudent and being self-controlled...

Let's look at this quality of life a bit closer. Paul's encouragement to *live soberly* means "To act in a responsible manner, sensibly, prudent and being self-controlled." Anna was determined to live such a life as this. How could she most wisely use her time, abilities and gifts? She discovered it in the presence of God before Him day and night. This was the challenge that I faced now that Jesus was living in my life and being filled with His Holy Spirit. How would I respond to such a transformational event that took place? It seemed as if for the first time in my life I had been awakened to something new and fresh, and it captured my entire being. What shape would my life take if by the Spirit's help I began living a *self-controlled* life (a fruit of the Spirit see Galatians 5:23). How would I respond academically? How would I use my time, abilities and gifts? How would I begin to live responsibly before the Lord and others as I sought to live out this new life in the Spirit?

Paul calls us to engage ourselves to live *righteously*. It is that quality of life that God imparts to us because it is the makeup of His character and nature. We have been delivered from one kingdom and have been transferred to another kingdom (Colossians 1:13); from darkness to light and from death to life, "Who called us out of darkness into His marvelous light" (1 Peter 2:9). I had to answer the question: How am I going to live? Paul in his letter to Titus describes it this way, "Not by works of righteousness which we have done, but according to His mercy He saved us, through the washing of regeneration (take away our sin NLT added) and renewing of the Holy Spirit" (3:5). The word *renewing*

Spirit-Filled Life Study Bible, Thomas Nelson Publishers, Nashville, TN 1991, p.1863.

means "a renovation, restoration, transformation, and a change of heart and life." This is the work of God from the inside-out, that positions our heart to stand with Him fully clothed in the nature and character of Christ – righteous!

The next quality of life Paul exhorts us to live is *godly*. It gives the idea of reverence or awe. We stand amazed in His presence. We are overwhelmed by His goodness and grace that He lavishly pours out upon us. It describes the posture of heart that honors the things of God; that holds them in high esteem. Anna desired such a life as she lived before the Lord every day of her life since the death of her husband. In that day and culture it was normal for girls to marry early, as early as twelve to fifteen years of age. Fr. Frederick Manns observes, "From the age of twelve, to twelve and one half years, a young Jewish girl was able to be promised in marriage." If Anna married approximately at the age of thirteen and she had been married to her husband for seven years and was now eighty-four when she saw Jesus in the temple, this means that Anna would have prayed (and fasted) for nearly sixty-four years. Anna took responsibility to live before the Lord in a way that

---

Fr. Frederick, Manns, *Everyday Life in the Time of Jesus*. 20 Dec. 1999. 10 Oct. 2010
http://198.62.75.1/www1/ofm/mag/TSmgenB3.html

honored, reverenced and held in high esteem what God had called her to do and we would call this, living "godly."

Finally, Anna was doing what Paul envisioned all of us to do, "Looking for the blessed hope and glorious appearing of our great God and Savior Jesus Christ" (Titus 2:13). Anna looked for the reward of beholding the King of Kings and Lord of Lords (Revelation 19:16).

Anna was able to answer the question: Where am I going? I am going to find in the Lord a place in Him that is not free from adversity, challenges or hardships, but a place where His presence can be experienced, a place where joy inexpressible and full glory (1 Peter 1:8) can be found. You may find yourself drifting off course, or having to deal with the void that only God can fill, and the journey you find yourself on is not leading you into that place of intimacy, fulfillment and joy in Christ. The call from our Lord to "draw near" (James 4:8) is offered to all who desire to do so. Anna not knowing where to go following the death of her husband, drew near to God and found her fulfillment in Him. As she prayed for the revelation, the unveiling, of the Son of

> In my heart of hearts I knew there was more but it was so illusive.

God to all humanity, she "Beheld His glory, as the glory of the only begotten of the Father, full of grace and truth" (John 1:14).

The last question we want to entertain is: "Who am I?" That is the powerful question many people ask, not just what is my function or what part do I play in life, but who am I. When no one is looking, when I am by myself, who am I? Many look in various places to discover who they are. Some set out to define who they are by what they do, the accomplishments they achieve and by the things they have gained. Anna could describe well who she was, "I am a prophetess (I have the God given ability to speak on behalf of God to others, added). I am the daughter of Phanuel, of the tribe of Asher" (Luke 2:36). The territory Asher received (upon coming into the Promised land as described in Joshua 19:24) was the fertile soil of the Mediterranean basin, which produced world renowned olive groves and helped them to become very prosperous. That is the lineage and pedigree from which Anna came and she could have declared that this was who she was. Yet, she found something much larger. She lived her days carrying out the divine assignment given to her by the Lord, to pray for the coming of the Son of God, Jesus. There was no higher calling she could undertake as praying for the birthing of the Son of God

Fulfilling Our Primary Purpose

and for her eyes to behold the glory of the Lord in the face of Jesus Christ (2 Corinthians 3:18).

I struggled with that question most of my life, who am I? Knowing the setbacks, disappointments and challenges to overcome, which seemed at the time very negative, but turned out to be a blessing (See Romans 8:28). The Apostle Paul describes that work in us, "For our light affliction, which is but for a moment, is working for us a far more exceeding and eternal weight of glory" (2 Corinthians 4:17). Those fateful words spoken by my fifth grade teacher, "By the time you are sixteen you will be either six foot under or behind bars" was almost fulfilled on that tragic night as I made my way to the highway. I was sixteen at the time. Yet, approximately six weeks later I found in Jesus a love, acceptance and a purpose I had never known before. Paul describes it this way, "Therefore, if anyone is in Christ, he is a new creation; old things have passed away; behold, all things have become new" (2 Corinthians 5:17). What was meant for evil God turned to good (Genesis 50:20). What the enemy seeks to do as Jesus describes, "The thief (devil added) does not come except to steal, and to kill, and to destroy. I have come that they may have life, and that they may have it abundantly" (John 10:10). Jesus made me a new person, the old man passed away (See Romans

6:6) and the new man was birthed (Colossians 3:10). There was a death that took place at the age of sixteen, the death of the old man and God made me into a new creation. I was now fulfilling God's divine assignment instead of those ill spoken words of another. Jesus said about Himself, "Therefore if the Son makes you free, you shall be free indeed" (John 8:36). For the first time in my life I experienced a freedom in Christ, not to be ruled by condemning thoughts, by shame and embarrassment, but I now had a new picture of who I am, who I belong to and the destiny and purpose that God placed into my heart and would now be launched forward to see what God would do as I offered myself to Him.

Anna, the prophetess shows us the importance of discovering our primary purpose in the quiet place, in solitude and listening to the voice of our heavenly Father. Having come out of that time of impartation, vision and character development we come forth as burning bushes, declaring the goodness, grace and love of God in Jesus Christ. It is in the hidden place where our significance becomes clear and our purpose is identified. We find our significance in Jesus Christ. We place ourselves under the mighty hand of God. We declare that we are sons and daughters of our heavenly Father.

May God's rich blessings be poured upon you as

Chapter 4
WHAT'S ALL THIS TALK ABOUT SPIRITUAL WARFARE?

I quickly discovered when I was going in the same direction as our enemy, the devil (also called our Adversary), that I had no problems. It was only after my decision to follow Christ that problems arose and now I had to make decisions based on what would bring glory to Jesus Christ. I remember going to a friend of mine and saying that I had invited Jesus Christ into my life and the way I was living had to change. I shared my recent experience with the love of Jesus Christ and asked him if he would like to give his life to Christ also. We had a prayer together, but he chose to wait to do anything about that. That person remained a friend, but I chose to go the way of Christ and found that He would surround me with another group of friends that held the same values and encouraged me in my new found faith in Jesus Christ.

I also discovered that the enemy, the devil, would seek to use my past against me from walking out my purpose and destiny in Christ. It would be through discouraging thoughts, shame, embarrassment, guilt, condemnation and habit patterns that had become engrained into the attitudes about life, others, my future and much of the time lived in a world of escapism. I discovered that God would have to change my thinking before I could begin to move forward. I had to deal with those words, "By the time you are sixteen you will either be six foot under or behind bars." God would have to deal with my self-esteem having being held back in school. I found out that the enemy is out to ruin our lives and he will use whatever tactics to accomplish his plans which are, "...to kill, steal and destroy" (John 10:10). I discovered that our enemy has "no truth in him. When he speaks a lie, he speaks from his own resources, for he is a liar and the father of it" (John 8:44). I had to make a choice, to

> God would have to deal with my self-esteem having being held back in school.

What's All This Talk About Spiritual Warfare?

believe the lie or to believe the truth that would "Set me free" (John 8:32). I chose to believe the truth!

I discovered that the word of God is able to stand against the forces of the enemy, to combat every ploy, plot and scheme that the enemy would use to take me off course, to discourage me or to hold me back from fulfilling God's design for my life. Claudio Freidzon shares this powerful story and illustrates God's redemptive work in our lives: "For seven years my congregation stayed at seven people. During some worship services I was completely alone; not even my wife could be present...I used to walk among the empty chairs as the devil laughed and whispered, 'You're no good; you'll never make any progress; it will always be like this.'" Claudio made this discovery in the midst of disappointment, shame, anger and confusion, "I thank God for my deserts. During those long years in the desert I battled my pride, my shyness, my limitations. My deserts are part of the roots of my walk with Christ. I could never disown them. In my desert, little by little God was teaching me that He is the only fountain." I discovered in the years of my desert that the enemy would speak words of defeat and hopelessness into my

---

Claudio Freidzon, *Holy Spirit, I Hunger For You*, Creation House, Lake Mary, FL, 1997, pp.14, 25 & 26.

life and speak to me about my limitations, but learned that the desert years are part of the roots of my walk with Christ. It would be the years that God would use to build His story into my life and, of His ability, change our weakness into His strength.

BEGINNING THIS NEW ADVENTURE OF LIVING THE SPIRIT-FILLED LIFE I WAS IN A BATTLE AND DISCOVERED FOUR TRUTHS

TRUTH #1 |

First truth, that "If God is for us, who can be against us...who would separate me from the Love of God...Yet in all these things we are more than conquerors through Him who loved us" (Romans 8:31, 35 and 37). I was reading the Bible from a paraphrase *Good News for Modern Man.* As a young believer, I would sit for hours drinking in God's word; I could not get enough of His word. I discovered my thinking, my attitudes and my perspective on life were beginning to change. The negativism was turning into faith.

TRUTH #2 |

Once I understood that God is for me and desired the best for my life, I discovered *a second truth,* "That the weapons of our warfare are not carnal, but mighty for

What's All This Talk About Spiritual Warfare?

pulling down strongholds," (2 Corinthians 10:4). I was learning to cast down arguments and every high thought that exalts itself against the knowledge of God. I was learning to bring every thought captive to the obedience of Christ (2 Corinthians 10:5). When negative, condemning and lying words of the enemy came flooding into my mind, I learned to take them captive and to send them back to the place where they originated – the pits of hell!

Terry Teykl, evangelist and author, defines strongholds, "As a belief system – a pattern of thinking, attitudes and expectation – that influences behavior and invites spiritual domination." We also find Ed Silvoso defines stronghold as "a mind-set impregnated with hopelessness that causes us to accept as unchangeable, situations that we know are contrary to the will of God." We see from these definitions, the destructive influence of the devil. In my life, God had to

> **I was learning to bring every thought captive to the obedience of Christ.**

Terry Teykl, *Divine Strongholds*, Prayer Point Press, Muncie, Indiana, 2008, p. 25, 37.

Ed Silvoso, *That None Should Perish*, Regal Books, Ventura, CA 1994, p.155.

deal with deep rooted rejections, suppressed anger and failure. The things that looked hopeless had become entrenched in my mind and a belief system circulated that things would not get any better. I had to replace the demonic stronghold for the spiritual stronghold of the Lord. The Psalmist declares, "The Lord is my rock and my fortress and my deliverer; My God, my strength, in whom I will trust; My shield and the horn of my salvation, my stronghold" (18:2). Terry Teykl explains, "To see divine strongholds grow in our midst, we must choose to put on the mind of Christ; we must make conscious decisions to tear down old ways of thinking and cut new grooves that reflect kingdom thinking." God had to deal with my stinking thinking and help me to believe that with Him nothing was impossible as Jesus said, "I say to you, if you have faith as a mustard seed you will say to this mountain, 'Move from here to there,' and it will move; and nothing will be impossible for you" (Matthew 17:20). Steve Fry observes, "But our Father in heaven promises to renew our minds, heal our hearts, and free us from the inner strongholds, which his friend Dan Sneed defines as, 'Negative thought patterns that are so strongly etched on our minds, they govern our

---

Steve Fry, *Rekindled Flame*, Multnomah Publishers, Sisters, OR, 2002, p. 84.

entire thinking process.'" The Lord had to deliver me from one thinking process to an entirely new vocabulary about life, about purpose and about myself that would be refreshing and totally new.

TRUTH #3 |

The third truth I was applying to my life, "There is therefore now no condemnation to those who are in Christ Jesus, who do not walk according to the flesh, but according to the Spirit" (Romans 8:1). The past could not haunt me any longer. The thoughts and attitudes that declared I was a failure, and a loser, were being broken off of my life. Now they were being replaced with the growing knowledge of who I am in Christ. The presence and power of Christ was becoming more real each day, as I was allowing His life-giving word and His Spirit access into my heart and mind.

TRUTH #4 |

The fourth truth I was learning was the importance of putting on the armor of God as described in Ephesians 6:14-17, "Stand therefore, having girded your waist with truth, having put on the breastplate of righteousness, and having shod your feet with the preparation of the gospel of peace; above all, taking the shield of faith with which you will be able to quench all the fiery darts of the wicked one. And take the helmet of salvation, and the sword of the Spirit, which is the word of God." Putting on the armor of God allows us to stand against the enemy's attack to take us off course, to weaken our witness, to discourage us and to steal God's purpose and destiny from our lives.

> ...the armor of God allows us to stand against the enemy's attack.

PUTTING ON THE ARMOR OF GOD ALLOWS US TO DO THREE THINGS

First we can wage a good warfare. Paul writes to Timothy, "This charge I commit to you...according to the prophecies made concerning you, that by them you may wage the good warfare" (1 Timothy 1:18). It allows us to declare and to claim the good promises of God He has for us. It gives us a frame of reference out of which we can live.

Second we are soldiers inducted into the army of God: "You therefore must endure hardship as a good soldier of Jesus Christ. No one engaged in warfare entangles himself with the affairs of this life, that he may

---

Spirit-Filled Life Study Bible, Thomas Nelson Publishers, Nashville, TN, 1991, p. 1793

please him who enlisted him as a soldier" (2 Timothy 2:3-4). The armor of God allows us to stand up under adversity, challenges of all sorts and discouraging thoughts and not to be sidetracked from fulfilling the purpose and calling of God upon our lives.

Third the armor of God allows us to resist the devil's plots, ploys and schemes. "Be sober, be vigilant; because your adversary the devil walks around like a roaring lion, seeking whom he may devour. Resist him...be steadfast in the faith" (1 Peter 5:8-9a). The armor of God equips us to be able to resist the enemy and to stand fast in the faith.

> ...the armor of God allows us to resist the devil's plots, ploys and schemes....

We find in Mark 5:1-20, an illustration of how the enemy seeks to rob our lives of the abundant life we have in Jesus Christ. Mark describes the life of a tomb dweller who was a cast off from society, who acted with hostility, isolating himself because of his hurts, wounds and destructive behavior. We would say he had strongholds in his life, and had a life transforming experience with Jesus.

WE DISCOVER THERE WAS A SENSE OF HOPELESSNESS THAT HELD THIS MAN CAPTIVE

"Because he had often been bound with shackles and chains...neither could anyone tame him and always, night and day, he was in the mountains and in the tombs, crying out and cutting himself with stones. When he saw Jesus from afar, he ran and worshiped Him" (Mark 5:4-6). I believe this man wanted to worship the Lord, but the enemy had a greater place in him than did the Lord. There was so much junk and excess baggage in his life that he was not able to worship the Lord, "in Spirit and in truth" (John 4:24). Ephesians 4:26 exhorts us, "...Be angry, and do not sin:'" do not let the sun go down on your wrath, nor give place (opportunity, added) to the devil." The word *place* (Gk. topos) means to give ground in our lives to the devil, our arch-enemy. It is not just *the devil made me do it,* but the disobedience that gives the enemy room, a place to invade areas in our lives that are not surrendered to the Lord.

This man had to get rid of some stuff before he could worship the Lord with all his heart. When we harbor anger, resentment, bitterness, unforgiveness, pride, rebellion, deception, sexual impurity and ungodly activities in our lives, we are giving *place* to the enemy;

giving him opportunity to gain control over our lives versus the Lord gaining control over our lives.

The foothold of the enemy was greater than the *place* or room the Lord occupied and that is the reason he said, "What have I to do with you, Jesus, Son of the Most High God?" (Mark 5:7). Isaiah the Prophet explains it this way, "But your iniquities have separated you from your God; and your sins have hidden His face from you, so that He will not hear" (59:2). The enemy had this man so bound that he was unable to fulfill God's purpose and destiny in his life. The shame he felt caused him to withdraw from society. The rejection he experienced was more than he could deal with and so he lived in isolation. The healing he needed could only be brought by the healing hand of Jesus Christ and His delivering words.

THE FREEDOM THAT ONLY CHRIST COULD BRING

Then they came to Jesus, and saw the one who had been demon-possessed and had the legion, sitting and clothed and in his right mind. And they were afraid (Mark 5:15). Jesus said, "If the Son sets you free, you are free indeed" (John 8:36). Peter in his Epistle declares those who have been transformed by the power of Jesus

---

Spirit-Filled Life Study Bible, Thomas Nelson Publishers, Nashville, TN, 1991, p. 1742.

Christ, "That you may proclaim the praises of Him who called you out of darkness into His marvelous light" (1 Peter 2:9). The question is: Do we want the Lord's freedom more than the enemy's bondage in our lives? Do we want to give a greater place to the Lord in our lives; more than any place the enemy would seek to gain?

> What would it take for God to set us free from things that inhibit [God].

What would it take for God to set us free from those things that inhibit the activity of God's Spirit working in and through us? I choose freedom over bondage, slavery and darkness. How about you?

Let me summarize what has happened to this man who was bound by sin and destructive habit patterns. He was:

† *Sitting* (Filled with the peace of God).
† *Clothed* (Shame is replaced with restored dignity).
† *In his right mind* (Thinking clearly - Having the mind of Christ).

Dale Evrist, *The Mighty Hand of God*, Creation House, Lake Mary, FL, 2000, p.208.

Steve Fry, *Rekindled Flame*, Multnomah Publishers, Sisters, OR, 2002, p. 84.

What's All This Talk About Spiritual Warfare?

Those who had seen this wonderful freedom saw how the tomb dweller had been transformed. "They also who had seen it told them by what means he who had been demon-possessed was [delivered]" (Luke 8:36). The word *healed* is also used for salvation or wholeness. This word describes Jesus' concern to restore every part of this man's life. That includes our relationship with God the Father, our broken personalities and bondages, our physical health and ultimately our rescue from death itself at the resurrection. Jesus Christ is the Savior of the whole man. The salvation and wholeness that only God can bring had truly changed this man's life.

There are two observations we can make about the community in which this miracle took place – the healing of a man held captive by the devil is now living proof of Christ's liberating power.

First, the fear that asked Jesus to leave. "Then the whole multitude...asked Him to leave, for they were seized with great fear" (Luke 8:37). Fear of the unknown had seized their hearts. What we do not understand we seek to dismiss, discredit and disparage.

Second, the response of the owners of the pigs and the community from the economic loss they experienced was astounding. They were more concerned about their loss than overjoyed by the one who had been held captive by the violent and destructive behavior of the enemy. So they asked Jesus to leave. They became so uncomfortable in the presence of the one who had been transformed by the power of Jesus Christ that they did not know what to do with Him. Transformed people make religious people uncomfortable. The bottom line is, they would rather have a man be in bondage and slavery to the devil, than to give up their pigs.

Finally, there is the devotion of the man to follow Jesus. "The man...begged that he might be with Jesus..." (Mark 5:18). Jesus said, "Go home to your friends, and tell them what great things the Lord has done for you, and how He has had compassion on you" (Mark 5:19). Out of this freedom comes devotion to be with Jesus and to cultivate a vital relationship with the One who changed his life forever. Watch the sequence of events as they unfold:

† Jesus accepts us as we are, but loves us too much to leave us as we are.

† Jesus sets the captive free so that we can wholeheartedly follow the Lord.

† Jesus gave him an assignment- "Go home to your family and friends."

Spirit-Filled Life Study Bible, Thomas Nelson Publishers, Nashville, TN, 1991, p. 1797.

What's All This Talk About Spiritual Warfare?

† Following Jesus requires obedience -"And he departed and began to proclaim..."
† Jesus told him to demonstrate the transformed life - "Tell them what great things the Lord has done for you and how He had compassion on you."
† Jesus loves our devotion to be with Him and so He sends us out as transformed and empowered witnesses in His name.
† Jesus is the lover of our soul and He wants room, the place in our lives exclusively given over to Him so that nothing else would hinder us in our fellowship with Him. I personally discovered that God brings us out of darkness, exposes our need for Him and sets us free to know and follow Him.

> Jesus is the lover of our soul and He wants room...

THREE STRATEGIES OF SPIRITUAL WARFARE

The outline can be found in James 4:7-8 "Therefore submit to God. Resist the devil and he will flee from you. Draw near to God and He will draw near to you." So the three areas of focus will be *"Submitting to God," "Resisting the devil"* and *"Drawing near to God."* These three truths will add to the already discussed ways in which spiritual warfare can take place.

Journey in Discipleship

STRATEGY #1 |

First of all, we struggle with the word "submit," because it has been misused and abused. But, let's examine it in relationship to submitting ourselves to God and getting an understanding of this principle. The word *submit* means "to stand under" and this word suggests obedience. I think this is one of the most powerful images that God gives us, as Peter describes, "Therefore humble yourselves under the mighty hand of God" (1 Peter 5:6). I discovered that I could live life my way or God's way. I can either *submit* or "stand under" His purpose for my life or I can choose to miss His best for me. Humbling ourselves under the mighty hand of God means getting His assignment for our lives; it means allowing Him to direct our lives and it means we are saying "yes" to His plans. Submitting to God is not a dirty word, but a liberating word. It helps me to realize that I am not on my own. I am surrounded by God's mighty hand that will not let me go or in no way loosen His grip upon my life.

Again, Steve Fry makes this comment about submitting our lives to Jesus, "We need to say to the Holy Spirit, 'I yield myself to you in this moment of

---

Spirit-Filled Life Study Bible, Thomas Nelson Publishers, Nashville, TN, 1991, p. 1793.

decision. I want only that which will glorify Jesus.' By doing this, we align ourselves with the great aim of the Holy Spirit, and that is to exalt Jesus." Submitting to God is a choice we make. Dale Evrist asks this powerful question, "Have you ever submitted to the shaping work of God in your life?" He goes on to make this your prayer, "Lord, You are my Maker. I will not strive with You. I will submit to You and I will submit to the work that You have to do in my life. I believe that You are making a masterpiece, whether or not it looks that way to me or to anyone else right now." The truth I discovered as I was doing spiritual warfare over the enemy's destructive way was that God is working on me. I am a masterpiece of God's handiwork and He never creates junk. Jeremiah tells the people of God, "If you still remain in this land, (don't let the enemy run you out, added), then I will build you and not pull you down, and I will plant you and not pluck you up. I will relent concerning the disaster that I have brought upon you" (42:10).

When we submit ourselves to God:
- † He *builds* us up. He encourages us. He gives us a foundation upon which to build.
- † He *plants* us for the purpose of bringing forth fruitfulness.
- † He *makes* it a place of restoration and not disaster.

Let us give ourselves fully and freely to our Lord Jesus Christ, allowing Him access into every area of our lives, so that we will be able to "Stand against the schemes" (Ephesians 6:11) of the enemy; all because we have learned to, submit, "Stand under" His authority and Lordship.

Joshua illustrates what it takes in leading the people of God into the promise land with an overcoming faith that submits to the mighty hand of God. Joshua asks two vital questions when he is confronted by the angel: "Are you for us or against us? And what does my Lord say to his servant? Take your sandal off your foot, for the place where you stand is holy" (Joshua 5:13-15). Joshua had to submit to that powerful command in order to see the fruition of God's plan for His people. James in his Epistle observes, "When you bow down before the Lord and admit your dependence on Him, He will lift you up and give you honor" (4:10). Again, Peter speaks of the necessity of standing under the authority of God. This is the key to promotion, blessing and provision. "Therefore humble yourselves under the

> Let us give ourselves fully and freely to our Lord Jesus Christ…

mighty hand of God that He may exalt you in due time" (1 Peter 5:6).

Submitting ourselves to the mighty hand of God indicates:

† Our *dependence* upon the Lord.
† Our *obedience* to what He calls us to.
† Our *ability* to stay the course in the midst of adversity.
† That God is *weaving* something precious, valuable, and eternal into the fabric of our life.
† That God gives us *grace* to stand in the midst of adversity.
† That God is *increasing* the measure of our faith through obedience.

A believer who has a faith that overcomes is one who submits to the mighty hand of God; who stands, thrives and increases in the midst of trials, testing and adversity; who knows that God is faithful and watches over His word to see that it is fulfilled in His way, in His time and in the way He wants to do it. We simply say, "Yes, Lord!"

STRATEGY #2 |

The second strategy of spiritual warfare is to, "Resist the devil (the enemy, our adversary, added) and he will flee" (James 4:7b). The word *resist* suggests "vigorously opposing, bravely resisting, standing face-to-face against an adversary; standing your ground." We not only are called to "Submit to God," but we are also called to "Resist the devil." Submitting to God suggests a defensive move. When the children of Israel made their escape from the tyranny and oppression of Pharaoh's regime, they plundered the enemy on their way out. The enemy chased them and Moses instructed the people of God, "Do not be afraid. Stand still, and see the salvation of the Lord, which He will accomplish for you today. The Egyptians you see today, you shall see again no more forever" (Exodus 14:13). They were standing for the One who was their Defender. The Psalmist declares, "But the salvation of the righteous is from the Lord; He is their strength in the time of trouble. And the Lord shall help them and deliver them; He shall deliver them from the wicked, and save them, because they trust in Him" (37:39-40). Whereas, the word *Resist* suggests an offensive move; it is something we do. It is an action or

---

Spirit-Filled Life Study Bible, Thomas Nelson Publishers, Nashville, TN, 1991, p.1797.

actions we take. I discovered in this spiritual warfare that I not only needed to bring every thought captive to the obedience of Christ, but I also had to continue to resist the enemy's schemes as Jack Hayford explains, "The adversary still contends for earth-rule, and until Christ finally expels all his workings, his conquest is experienced only through warfare. Each believer is a member of an occupational force which has one principle purpose: to enforce the victory of Calvary." I discovered to resist is more than a one time event; it is keeping your guard up all the time. I am constantly on the offensive – resisting! Jesus described it this way, "And from the days of John the Baptist until now the kingdom of heaven suffers violence, and the violent take it by force" (Matthew 11:12). There is violent response by the believer to enforce the reign and rule of Christ on earth and in their lives as we resist the devil and his schemes.

  David understood the necessity of resisting the enemy who comes as a roaring lion seeking those whom he may devour. David shouted to the giant, "You come to me with sword, spear, and javelin, but I come to you in the name of the Lord Almighty...And everyone will know that the Lord does not need weapons to rescue His

---

Jack W. Hayford, *Prayer is Invading the Impossible*, Bridge-Logos Publishers, North Brunswick, NJ, 1977 revised 2000, p. 18.

people. It is His battle, not ours. The Lord will give you to us" (1 Samuel 17:45-47).

† No matter what the enemy throws at us, God is greater still. For the weapons of our warfare are mighty in God, for the pulling down of every stronghold.

† There is a name given that is above every name, and at His name every knee shall bow and every tongue shall confess that Jesus Christ is Lord.

† God fights for us, the battle is the Lord's – we only need to stand and see the salvation of the Lord. If God be for us, who can be against us? The battle is not ours, but God's.

STRATEGY #3 |

The third strategy of spiritual warfare is "Draw near to God." The promise is God will "Draw near to us" (James 4:8). To draw near is a choice, a decision to do the opposite of what the enemy is telling us through the bombardment of thoughts and actions that do not honor or glorify God. In drawing near, I am getting closer to the heart of God, to His thoughts, to His actions and to His will. As I was learning to draw near to God, I found I was drawing upon His resources, His wisdom, His strength and His presence.

What's All This Talk About Spiritual Warfare?

One of the books that God placed in my hands early in my new life in Christ was entitled *Perfect Everything* by Rufus Mosley. He described such a deep and intimate relationship with Jesus that it caused a great hunger and desire to draw near to Jesus. Mosley described how we could walk in such an intimate relationship to Jesus as we drew near to God. God puts things in our hands that cause us to draw near, to thirst after Him and for Him to fill us completely with Himself so that there is room for nothing else, but Jesus.

FOUR REASONS WE CAN DRAW NEAR TO GOD

REASON #1 |

First, because we need His guidance. The people of God asked the prophet to pray for them, "That the Lord your God may show us the way in which we should walk and the thing we should do" (Jeremiah 42:2-3). We don't know the way we should go, or what we are to be about doing, so let us draw near that we might understand, comprehend and resolve to do. Because in our drawing near we receive the heart of the Father; we are completely dependent upon Him.

REASON #2 |

Second, we can draw near because it is good to do so as the Psalmist writes, "But it is good for me to draw near to God" (73:28). It is good because we are proactive in seeking the heart and mind of Christ. It is good to seek the presence of God as David records in Psalm 27:4, "One thing I have desired of the Lord, that I will seek: that I may dwell in the house of the Lord all the days of my life and to behold the beauty of the Lord." Drawing near becomes our passion!

REASON #3 |

Third, we can draw near because it is God who creates within us a clean and pure heart, "Who may ascend into the hill of the Lord? Or who may stand in His holy place? He who has clean hands and a pure heart" (Psalms 24:3-4). We can draw near to God because Christ cleanses us from our sin and from those things that separate us from Him. We can draw near "lifting up holy hands" to the Lord (1 Timothy 2:8). We can draw near in worship and praise lifting our hands in surrender of all ourselves to Him who is able to keep what we have committed to Him.

What's All This Talk About Spiritual Warfare?

REASON #4 |

Finally, we can draw near to God out of obedience to Him and we can draw near because we find Him to be our fortress, our deliverer, our strength, our shield, our salvation and our stronghold (Psalm 91:1-2). To draw near is to draw upon His divine power as He has given to us all things that pertain to life and godliness (2 Peter 1:3).

We have examined this important subject on spiritual warfare and why it is important to each day put on the armor of God. I call it getting dressed spiritually. When our children were young, we made it a practice at breakfast just before the girls left for school to put on the armor of God. We would place the helmet of salvation on our head. We would put on the breastplate of righteousness. We would put on the belt of truth. We would put on shoes of the gospel of peace. Finally, we would take up the shield of faith and take up the sword of the Spirit. We did this until they were old enough to do it for themselves.

Let me encourage you to get dressed spiritually each day as you put on the armor of God – I don't leave home without it!

May God's rich blessings be poured upon you as you live the Spirit-filled life. I invite you to engage yourself and others, and apply the truths and principles found in the study guide section titled, *What's All This Talk about Spiritual Warfare,* found in the back of the book (p.227-242).

Chapter 5
WHEN IT COMES TO SPIRITUAL DIRECTION - I'M CHALLENGED.

We found ourselves without a home, furniture, salary and no place to pastor. I had been serving as a pastor in the United Methodist Church for sixteen years, and my last assignment was planting a new church. We were using Carl George's book *Prepare Your Church for the Future*. Our principal method of growing was through celebration and cells (small groups) as our means of connecting people and growing as a church. In January of 1990, we launched our first service with approximately a hundred and fifty-seven people. We had been meeting for nearly three years and up to that point I was spending most of my time with cell leaders and their apprentices, encouraging and equipping them to be effective cell group leaders. I discovered my life had gotten out of balance and church planting was becoming more than I had bargained for. I was being driven by the approval of others, feeling the need to succeed and the pressure I personally placed upon myself. And so, I deviated from what I had learned early on in my walk with Christ about living the Spirit-filled life and being lead by the Holy Spirit. I was asking the Lord, *What shall I do?* I felt overwhelmed and burned out. I approached our Bishop and shared with him that everything was in place: quality worship service, Sunday school classes, children's church and cell groups had been established and doing well. I shared with him the need to step down and get out from under the pressure cooker. He felt because the church was so young, I needed to stay. That was not what I wanted to hear, but I understood the point he was making. It was in July of 1993 as I approached the podium that Sunday morning that I said to the congregation, "The leadership needs for you to embrace the vision that is being cast. If you are not able to embrace that vision, you need to find a place where you can embrace that vision and run with it." It would be the next to the last sermon I would preach at that church. I was immediately asked to step down by the District Superintendent and to take a month off before returning. I used that month to focus on the Lord and to refresh myself in Him. I spent time with family

When It Comes to Spiritual Direction – I'm Challenged.

and friends and asked the Lord, *What are you saying in all of this?* I would go on long walks praying and worshiping the Lord and looking to see what He was saying. During that time my wife and I heard the same word spoken by six different people at different times, "You will be like Abraham and Sarah. You will leave your country, your people and I will take you where you have not known before" (Genesis 12:1 and Hebrews 11: 8). We concluded that God might be saying something to us, but we had nowhere to go. Yet out of obedience we left. I turned in my ordination and received an honorable discharge by our Bishop.

> We discovered again and again how God was our Provider.

We were launched into a journey that would cover a period of twelve years. We found by taking that step of obedience, God would meet us. We were provided with a four bedroom house and enough furniture to fill it up. I found employment outside the pastorate and we would periodically go out to the mailbox and find envelopes with twenty dollar bills in it from unknown sources. We discovered again and again how God was our Provider. My wife and I looked forward to each week when we went to worship to count up what God had provided us with that week so we could tithe from it.

    I don't know about you, but when it comes to spiritual direction – I'm challenged. After all is said and done, it is about obedience. I took a staff position in a church for a year and allowed the Lord to continue to speak to us and to discern what He was saying and to interpret what it meant to leave one place and find ourselves going where we had never gone before. I was a teacher and an administrator of a Bible Institute. But once again we found ourselves being pushed from the nest and back into church planting, but doing it in a different way. This time, we were not driven by human achievement, but we were led by the Holy Spirit. My wife and I drove through three areas, and as we drove through those areas, we sensed the presence, direction and witness of the Holy Spirit to plant a church in that area. I discovered the importance and power of prayer as one discerns the will and purpose of God. I remember walking through the entire town praying over the businesses, churches and subdivisions asking God's blessing, provision and if there were those who did not know Jesus, that they would come to know Him. We would set up either at the local YWCA or in the conference room of one the motels in town. We

When It Comes to Spiritual Direction – I'm Challenged.

discovered a new paradigm for doing church – it was in the house! I remember at one point we had fifty people meeting regularly in our home for worship, fellowship, teaching and meals together. I discovered I was just as comfortable in the house as I was in the pulpit preaching to people lined up in pews.

Then came a period in my life where going back was easier than moving forward. I could really identify with the people of Israel as they longed for the leeks and melons of Egypt, than to press through the emotions and do the necessary spiritual warfare to keep pressing upward and onward. Yet, I had surrounded myself with the larger region of spiritual leadership for prayer, support and encouragement. We had completed six years of ministry where we had planted this work and it kept going down in attendance. I was confused, frustrated and ready to make a change. It was at this point where spiritual direction got a bit unclear. I needed to wait for the next step, since the Lord did say, *I will take you where you have not known before.* Sometimes, we get impatient and get ahead of the Lord; we even seek to make things happen. This leads me to share a story about a side trip we took that didn't end well. I called a good pastor friend of mine whom I had met while planting the Methodist church in Knoxville, TN. He had moved to Florida and I called to ask if there were any churches in his denomination that were looking for a pastor. He invited me to come and serve on staff with him and give leadership to their small group ministry and help out in other areas of ministry. I should have picked up early on that this was going to be a rocky time. The church where we were going to minister had flown us down to meet us and to extend to us an opportunity to share with them our faith in Jesus Christ and God's call upon our life. On our way back to McGhee Tyson Airport in Knoxville, TN we arrived in one of the hardest rainstorms I had been in while flying. Thunder and lightning was striking all about the plane. My wife and I were sitting in separate places on the plane because it was full and we were unable to get seats together. The fear, anxiety and the unknowing was terrifying. Seeking spiritual direction from the Lord should have caused us to ask the question, *Is God saying something to us through this storm?* Our spiritual radar to discern God's direction had taken a back seat. I was more intent in getting to the next place than in correctly discerning God's will and purpose of our lives.

When It Comes to Spiritual Direction – I'm Challenged.

Our youngest daughter and I set out for Florida and we were waiting for my wife to finish teaching school for that year. We would go early to look for a place to live and to begin working in the church. I had difficulty in finding and keeping a job. I was constantly having snake dreams. One snake dream I had was that every time I struck at it, it mutated. Our daughter and I were feeling the stress in our relationship, because things were not going as we thought they would. We could not find a place to live that we felt the peace of God about. Then suddenly everything came to a head. I made one of the greatest mistakes, without communicating to my pastor friend who had invited me to be on staff, without communicating to the church our decision and without communicating to the family we had spent three months with—we just left! I discovered I left in the wake of confusion, misunderstanding, hurt, disappointment and frustration. I left my pastor friend with the difficult task of picking up the pieces and sharing with the church we had just left – with no explanation at all. It was one of the lowest times in my life. A few days later, I drove back to Florida and met with my pastor friend to apologize and explain the best I could the actions I had taken. I don't know about you, but when it comes to spiritual direction

– I'm challenged. Let me share several things I took away from that experience.

A FEW THINGS I TOOK AWAY FROM THAT EXPERIENCE

† *First,* don't run from one place to another place until God is finished with you in the place where you presently are.

† *Second,* keep a keen ear out to what God might be saying to you in the circumstances in which you find yourself.

† *Third,* in my impetuous nature, I failed to really seek the Lord to see what He was saying as it relates to our next step.

† *Fourth,* the decisions we make have enormous consequences on others it has a ripple effect.

† *Fifth,* I discovered we can miss God, but He uses everything for our good and for His glory (Romans 8:28).

† *Sixth,* I failed to examine God's word and how He had led us up to that point and was consistent in His direction for our lives.

† *Finally,* God will bring us to a point of brokenness and repentance so that we might find in Him forgiveness, restoration and the ability to learn and keep moving. Yes, we made a mistake but it was not

When It Comes to Spiritual Direction – I'm Challenged.

the end. We learn, we grow, God matures us and we become even more dependent upon Him. We grow in our spiritual direction from the Lord.

Upon returning to the Knoxville area, the denomination we had been with was seeking to reach me concerning a church they wanted me to consider serving in Kentucky. We told them our family would stop on our way back from Toronto following our services at Toronto Airport Christian Fellowship. I preached at their Sunday morning service and they invited us to stay. We went back to Knoxville and prayed. We did not want to miss Him again. Missing Him is too painful. I was awakened the night we got back to our home in Knoxville and sensed that God was calling us to Kentucky. There was a group of folks that desired God and we felt Him in the midst of us in a mighty way. We had a small group that met in homes and found new ways to pray that ushered in the presence of the Holy Spirit. We discovered in this setting God was still doing some deep work in our lives, learning to trust one another again, learning to communicate what we sensed

> We went back to Knoxville and prayed. We did not want to miss Him again.

God was saying to us, and learning to connect again as a family. I knew in my spirit that God was not yet finished with us in the United Methodist Church. My wife was working for low income housing and there was a property she transferred to from Kentucky to Tennessee, just north of Knoxville. She was the property manager and I was hired as the Service Coordinator for a low income senior property. I helped with connecting the elderly with the different services, signing them up for food stamps, assisting with issues like Social Security and just making the property a safe place for them to live. There was a Methodist church next door to the property and the pastor would invite me to preach whenever he was out of town or on vacation. He encouraged me again and again to come back into the United Methodist church. I finally took the necessary steps and found open doors that were not there before. Shortly after making steps to return, the District Superintendent called and asked if I would preach at a couple of churches while the pastor recovered from a motorcycle accident. Our time with these churches was very confirming and encouraging. We continued our pursuit to return to the Methodist church with guarded expectations, so not to get ahead of the Lord. This same District Superintendent called and said they had a full

When It Comes to Spiritual Direction – I'm Challenged.

time appointment for me if I wanted it. It was interesting that my first Sunday was January 1, 2005. It was as if God was giving us a new start. It would be the door God opened for us to return and we found ourselves coming full circle after being out for twelve years. My wife and I never really thought we would return, but I had sensed deep in my spirit that God had not yet finished with us. We found our return to be quite challenging. We had been accustomed to opening worship with a worship leader and a band and, we were free to express ourselves in worship. Now we wondered if we had anything to offer. We found ourselves warmly welcomed by colleagues and friends I had made through the previous sixteen years in the Methodist church. But I quickly discovered that God has a sense of humor and we discovered "Never say, never!"

In our trek outside the Methodist church, we gained a wonderful son-in-law, three grandchildren, we met some wonderful people, we discovered how God is moving in other places, we learned to wait and bask in God's presence of renewing and refreshing, we learned that God is weaving through us a message and a testimony that honors and glorifies Him and we discovered that God will never leave us nor forsake us.

We discovered that in God's economy, He always provides for our every need. We learned the importance of walking in forgiveness and to walk in love and give it away. We learned that God is a great big God!

> We all come before the Lord vulnerable, weak and desperately needing His guidance.

Let's turn to a story of a man who was blind and needed a second touch from Jesus for his sight to be completely restored. We find this account in Mark 8:22-26. Let's examine *four important truths about spiritual direction* and God's touch upon our eyes that we may see Him and see what He is doing and saying.

FOUR IMPORTANT TRUTHS ABOUT SPIRITUAL DIRECTION
TRUTH #1 |

First of all, the blind man needed someone to lead him. "So He took the blind man by the hand and led him" (Mark 8:23). We all come before the Lord vulnerable, weak and desperately needing His guidance and direction for our lives. Isaiah addresses this issue as he hears the Lord say, "I will bring the blind by a way they did not know; I will lead them in paths they have not known. I will make darkness light before them"

When It Comes to Spiritual Direction – I'm Challenged.

(42:16). God says I will do three things: "I will bring...I will lead; I will make." These are all promises that God gives to His sons and daughters. God brings us to Himself that we might know His heart and His ways. Then, He leads us by the hand into places and in ways which we have not gone before. Finally, He will make a way because He is the way maker. Again, Isaiah observes, "Thus says the Lord who makes a way in the sea and a path through the mighty waters" (43:16). Our heavenly Father is the Way Maker! He makes a way where there is no way. Jesus really wants us to get this because He wants us to fulfill our purpose and destiny. He wants us to know that He can be trusted and would never lead His children in a way that would do them harm or discourage them in any way.

There was yet another truth the Lord was pressing upon me, before the Lord directs our steps, before He leads us in the right path. We have to come to the realization that we need to be led. After that heart wrenching experience in getting ahead of the Lord in our move to Florida, I came to the stark reality that I not only wanted God's guidance and leadership, but I now desperately needed His hand of blessing and guidance in our lives, even if it meant going back to the place where we began, where we first heard from God about where He wanted us to plant a new church. Sometimes we have to go back to the original word God gave to us and allow Him to speak to us again from the place we last heard His voice. We not only admit and confess our need for His direction, but we in humility and brokenness allow the Lord to take our hand and let Him gently affirm us as His sons and daughters, letting Him restore us to Himself and affirming us with His love. Sometimes instead of running to the Father, we run still further in the opposite direction trying to make something happen or compound our problem by making yet another presumptive decision and we find ourselves further from God's direction and guidance for our lives. Jesus said, "He calls His own sheep by name and leads them out" (John 10:3). God wants us to know that He is for us, not against us. We do not need to create our own fire. Isaiah instructs us about starting our own fires, "Look, all you who kindle a fire, who encircle yourselves with sparks; walk in the light of your fire and in the sparks you have kindled – this you shall have from My hand; you shall lie down in torment" (50:11). I understood the torment of walking out from under God's authority and His hand of blessing and provision. There was no peace, no joy and heaven seemed to be closed. This is what God was seeking to teach me in those times of seeming separation

When It Comes to Spiritual Direction – I'm Challenged.

from Him. Isaiah states it well, "Who among you fears the Lord? Who obeys the voice of his servant? Who walks in darkness and has no light? Let him trust in the name of the Lord and rely upon his God" (50:10). This is the truth the Lord was pressing upon me: learn to walk in the fear of the Lord, learn to trust Him and to rely upon His resources to lead, guide and to direct our ways.

TRUTH #2 |

The second truth about spiritual direction we find about this blind man in Mark 8:22-26 is he needed Jesus to lead him where he could not go by himself, "...And (Jesus added) led him out of the town" (8:23). There are some things Jesus has to lead us out of and into before He can do what He desires to do in us. Jesus is absolutely trustworthy and would never take us where it is not for our good and for His glory.

> Jesus is absolutely trustworthy and would never take use where it is not for our good and for His glory.

The phrase "...And led him out of the town," speaks of four principles about Jesus' leadership:

† It speaks of our dependence upon the Lord.

† It will require that we trust Him.

† It will demand our cooperation to His leading.

† It will demonstrate the necessity of childlike faith.

Now we are not sure why Jesus took this man who was blind out of town. Sometimes the place where we are is holding us back from experiencing God's breakthrough in our lives. Sometimes we have to go to another place where we experience different sounds, smells and expressions. Sometimes we have to go to different places where the atmosphere is different in order to experience a breakthrough. We experienced many of these as God led us out of the United Methodist church where God would do something in our hearts that He could not do elsewhere. We simply embrace God's extravagant grace and mercy. We can go anywhere as long as we know Jesus holds our hand. We will go with Him even though we cannot see clearly where He is taking us, but we know it will be for our good and for the shaping of Himself in us. Yet, even in the hard places Jesus fashions us to be more like Him. Jesus uses everything and wastes nothing. He uses our blunders to draw us to

When It Comes to Spiritual Direction – I'm Challenged.

Himself. He uses those times when we feel we missed Him, to show us how much we have missed Him and our fellowship with Him.

What a brave heart this man had for Jesus to take him out of his comfort zone, out of the sounds, smells, family, friends and familiar voices to a place he did not know. The one thing he knew was he wanted to see; and, at all cost he was willing to go to receive what only Jesus could give him – his sight! How we resist the kindness of Jesus because we are unwilling to move beyond our comfort zone, the sounds, smells and the familiar to get our sight.

TRUTH #3 |

The third truth about spiritual direction we find about this blind man, is that the blind man was willing for the Lord to do whatever it took to receive his sight. "And when he had spit on his eyes and put His hands on him, He asked him if he saw anything" (Mark 8:23). Was he asking him can you see through the saliva? Can you see the moisture of my spit? Don't you think it was a bit awkward? But again, this speaks of the man's childlike spirit, his ability to press through what must have been uncomfortable.

I remember how awkward it was returning to Florida to make amends for my actions or lack thereof. How I had to come face-to-face with my own story, my own shortcomings and my failures. I was embarrassed about what I had done; the lack of character that was shown and to see the disappointment on my friends' faces was most difficult. We talked about how from the get go the timing might have been wrong. We talked about where the congregation is going from here and how will they respond? We talked about how levels of trust and integrity had been violated and our friendship damaged. But, even in the midst of these emotions, we still allowed Jesus to apply something of Himself into our hurts, wounds and disappointments. We can hear the gentle voice of Jesus, *Do you see anything yet?* Jesus, all I see is what I have done and what could have been. Jesus inquires about us, where are you in your healing? And in your restoration to the Father's love? I see your healing hand upon me as my prayer is, "Behold, you desire truth in the inward parts, and in the hidden part you will make me know wisdom...Wash me and I shall be whiter than

> Jesus, all I see is what I have done and what could have been.

When It Comes to Spiritual Direction – I'm Challenged.

snow...Restore to me the joy of Your salvation and uphold me by Your generous Spirit" (Psalm 51:6, 8, 12).

Jesus asked that powerful question, *You see anything yet?* Well, I am beginning to see something. It is not completely clear, but it is getting there. I believe if you could just touch me one more time, the fullness of my sight shall return.

TRUTH #4 |

Jesus brought this man to a place where he realized he needed yet another touch, "Then He put His hands on his eyes again and made him look up. And he was restored and saw everything clearly" (Mark 8:25). There are areas in our lives that need a second, a third, or more of God's touch upon our lives. Not because His power is incapable of making us whole, but we may not be ready to receive all that God has for us and we need the continual drawing of the Holy Spirit to allow God to do yet deeper things in our lives. We find this to be true for Elisha's servant who was overwhelmed by the Syrians who had surrounded them. "Elisha prayed that the eyes of his servant would be opened, 'Lord, I pray, open his eyes that he may see.' Then the Lord opened the eyes of the young servant, and he saw. And behold the mountain was full of horses and chariots of fire all around Elisha (2 Kings 6:17)." God brings us to a place where we desire more. Jesus asked the blind man, *Do you see anything?* The blind man told him what he saw, but Jesus created in this man a desire to want more. His partial blindness caused him to want all of his sight restored. In receiving God's direction, something may not be completely clear, so keep asking for clarity of vision, to see clearly.

Upon returning and receiving an invitation to come to Kentucky, our spiritual vision was clearer but even there it was not the last word that God had for us. He would continually lead us in the right paths. We just needed to get on His page. The Lord had to touch our spiritual vision again and again until we got it.

We find this truth of spiritual vision, as God would once again touch the people of Israel, because God works with us until we get it.

"So thirty-eight years passed from the time we first arrived at Kadesh-barnea until we finally crossed Zered Brook" (Deuteronomy 2:14). God took them back to the place where they had to choose whose report they would believe. They would either believe the report of the ten who said there were giants living in the land, or believe the two who said, "The land is great and the Lord will fight for us and we will take the land just as the Lord

When It Comes to Spiritual Direction – I'm Challenged.

had declared" (Numbers 14:6-10). This was the opportunity for yet another touch of God upon the spiritual vision of the people of God.

God works with us for these reasons until we get it, and He releases new spiritual vision:

† Because God is building His character into our lives. "Knowing the testing of your faith produces endurance" (James 1:3).

† Because God is transforming us. "I feel as if I am going through labor pains for you again, and they will continue until Christ is fully formed in our lives" (Galatians 4:19).

> God touches our spiritual vision so that we can make small advances.

† Because God is developing our testimony. "I have prayed for you that your faith should not fail; and when you have returned to Me, strengthen your brethren" (Luke 22:32).

† Because God is imparting vision. "But one thing I do, forgetting those things which are behind and reaching forward to those things which are ahead" (Philippians 3:13).

God touches our spiritual vision so that we can make small advances.

"And the Lord your God will drive out those nations before you little by little; you will be unable to destroy them at once..." (Deuteronomy 7:22).

How does the Lord give us those small advances toward spiritual vision?

The apostles said to the Lord, "increase our faith" (Luke 17:5). "But also for this reason, giving all diligence, add to your faith..." (2 Peter 1:5). God desires that we be fruitful – it is the mark of discipleship. "Most assuredly, I say to you unless a grain of wheat falls into the ground and dies, it remains alone; but if it dies; it produces much grain" (John 12:24). "By this My Father is glorified, that you bear much fruit; so you will be My disciples" (John 15:8).

God wants us to really know Him. "But grow in the grace and knowledge of our Lord and Savior Jesus Christ" (2 Peter 3:18).

We discover these pivotal truths:
† God's desire is to restore spiritual vision.
† God delights in taking us by the hand and leading us where He wants to take us.
† God will deliver us from the familiar and the comfortable and take us to a new place in Him, because He loves us too much to leave us as we are

When It Comes to Spiritual Direction – I'm Challenged.

Because I seek to stay in tune with God's leadership and guidance, I am asking the Lord to open the eyes of my heart as Paul prayed for the church, "I pray that your hearts will be flooded with light so that you can understand the wonderful future he has promised to those he called. I want you to realize what a rich and glorious inheritance he has given to his people" (Ephesians 1:18 NLT). It is by continuously going to the "Father of lights" (James 1:17) who gives light to our paths and leads us in the right ways, "Come, people of Israel (believers, added), let us walk in the light of the Lord" (Isaiah 2:5 NLT). I have discovered that walking in the light of God's counsel is a learned trait. I have learned God's guidance comes as I am listening to the Holy Spirit, confirmed by His word.

We are on a journey and some of our trips are side trips, but we always take something away from those side trips. Most of all, there is a purity of heart that seeks the heart of the Father while on this journey and seeks to live a life of obedience before the Lord.

May God's rich blessings be poured upon you as you live the Spirit-filled life. I invite you to engage yourself and others, and apply the truths and principles found in the study guide section titled, *When it Comes to Spiritual Direction – I'm Challenged,* found in the back of the book (p.243-252).

Chapter 6
LEARNING TO PRAY IN THE POWER OF THE SPIRIT

I want to take this chapter to discuss the profound effect prayer has made upon my life. I invite you to journey with me in my discovery and understand this avenue of communicating with God called prayer. Following our time at Camp Farthest Out in which I was filled with the Holy Spirit, prayer began to be cultivated when our pastor's wife gathered the youth group together at the parsonage after school. Members of the youth group would also go to the sanctuary frequently and pray together. There was such a hunger and thirst for God and we longed for His presence. During Sunday evening worship service or Wednesday Bible study, the Spirit of God would come so strongly upon me and the joy of the Lord was so overwhelming that I could not contain it. I would begin to laugh and have to leave the service so as not to interrupt what was going on.

Spiritual relationships are undergirded by prayer. Paul writes to Timothy, "Without ceasing I remember you in my prayers night and day" (2 Timothy 1:3).

We forever live with this tension of Christian community and reaching out to those who are not yet Christians. George Hunter in his book, *To Spread the Power: Church Growth in the Wesleyan Spirit,* observed this about the ministry of John Wesley. In a journal entry of 1743 Wesley declares, "The devil himself desires nothing more than this, that the people of any place should be half-awakened and then left to themselves to fall asleep again. Therefore, I determine by the grace of God not to strike one stroke in any place where I cannot follow the blow." The principle is that Wesley declared with the general public the Good News of Jesus Christ, followed by building Christian community so that the new believers could grow and mature in their walk with Christ.

Early on in my new found faith in Jesus Christ I wanted to know what had awakened others to their need for Christ. What was the crisis or event that brought

---

George Hunter, *To Spread the Power: Church Growth in the Wesleyan Spirit,* p. 186.

them to Jesus? Like-mindedness means we are on a journey together and God is transforming our lives and we are becoming more and more like Jesus. Like-mindedness is allowing Jesus to so transform us that we have His mind. "Let this mind be in you that is in Christ Jesus..." (Philippians 2:5).

Leonard Sweet and Frank Viola in their book *Jesus Manifesto* describes well our single-minded purpose as believers in Jesus— "When Christ is not central and supreme in our lives, everything about life shifts out of orbit and moves out of kilter. So for Christians, our first task is to know Jesus. And out of that knowing, we will come to love Him, adore Him, proclaim Him, and manifest Him."

> I desire to develop authentic spiritual relationships..

I was sharing with a group of folks in our congregation about the kind of church I dreamed of: I dream of a church where we are moved by permission giving, that is, through the agreement of having prayed through what we sense God is saying to us, and moving forward towards God's vision for His Church. I dream of

---

Leonard Sweet and Frank Viola, *Jesus Manifesto,* Thomas Nelson, Nashville, TN, 2010, p. 2.

a church where people are coming to know the love of Jesus and experiencing the fullness of God's Spirit. I dream of a church where loving relationships are being developed through intentional small group ministry creating a culture of discipleship, evangelism and service. I dream of a church that is radical, filled with the new wine of the Spirit, the atmosphere is permeated with joy, laughter, lots of noise, and very contagious. The question becomes, "Can we agree on these things?" It is more than will these be our values, but will these things allow the life of Jesus to manifest Himself through this dream? Can our hearts and minds be connected to one another for such a dream to come to pass?

When I experienced God's unconditional love and acceptance, there was a desire to connect with others who had experienced Christ's unconditional love and acceptance. I wanted to hear their stories of what their journey was like before they knew Christ, after they had experienced Christ, and what difference He was making in their lives on a daily basis. I was learning we were "living stones being built up as a spiritual house" (1 Peter 2:5).

I was discovering that everyone has something to contribute to the Body of Christ, the church. I desired to develop authentic spiritual relationships and much of the time was spent in small group settings. That is why I believe in small groups of three to twelve people meeting on a regular basis for fellowship, discipleship, Bible study, and resulting in multiplication. It was where I experienced Christ in a real way.

I saw the transformation that took place when involved in small groups. One of the first books I read was *Brethren Hang Loose* by Robert C. Girard as he comments, in Acts 2:42-47, "The Lord added new converts to the church daily, but the reason for gathering together was so that those who were already believers could be taught by the Apostles, enjoy spiritual fellowship with one another, remember the Lord's death and its benefits by sharing in communion, and pray together."

PRINCIPLES OF PRAYING IN THE POWER OF THE SPIRIT
PRINCIPLE #1 | PRAY WITH PURPOSE

The objectives of praying with purpose are summarized by the following:

Terry Teykl in his book *Pray the Price* observes, "Authentic prayer is doing whatever it takes to invite the

---

Robert C. Girard, *Brethren Hang Loose*, Zondervan Publish House, Grand Rapids, MI, 1972, p. 81.

Terry Teykl, *Pray the Price*, Power Point Press, Muncie, IN, 1997.

kingdom of God to manifest itself here on the earth. E. Stanley Jones describes prayer, 'The first thing in prayer is to get God. If you get Him, everything else follows...allow God to get at you, to invade you, to take possession of you. He then pours His prayers through you. They are His prayers – God-inspired, and hence, God answered.'"

> Don't lay the purpose of God down for your life. Fight the enemy and all his cohorts...

WE FIND PRAYING WITH PURPOSE HAS FOUR ASPECTS

† *Know your purpose:* "...For this purpose the Son of God was manifested, that He might destroy the works of the devil" (1 John 3:8). The way to pray with a purpose is to know the purpose God has put into your heart. How can we know God's purpose? God's purpose for everyone is that all people come to a true knowledge of Christ as Savior and Lord of their life and to be filled with His Spirit and be conformed to the image of His Son, Jesus. Because God has created each human being differently, we seek the Lord however He wants to express Himself through us. Each of us has been given gifts, talents and abilities; and we use

those for the purpose of God's kingdom. Go into the secret place where you will find the Lord waiting for you and while you are there, ask Him what His purpose is for you and how that is to be expressed. Know your purpose!

† *Pray your purpose:* Jesus said, "Now My soul is troubled, and what shall I say? 'Father, save Me from this hour'? But for this purpose I came to this hour" (John 12:27). One of the most powerful things we can do once the Lord has spoken to us, even if it is a small piece of God's purpose, is to begin to pray into that purpose. Allow the Holy Spirit to breathe life into God's purpose for your life. If it is to teach, then begin asking God to fill you with that ability to communicate God's truths in such a way that people learn. If it is to be a businessperson, then ask God to give you favor with those with whom you do business and allow the Holy Spirit to give you inspired ideas and concepts. Jesus was able to fulfill His purpose, because He prayed into that purpose and realized the very purpose for which He came was to give His life so that we could know Him.

† *Possess your purpose*: that is, take ownership of God's purpose for your life. Jesus said, "The hour has come that the Son of Man should be glorified. Most

assuredly, I say to you unless a grain of wheat fall into the ground and dies, it remains alone, but if it dies, it produces much grain" (John 12:24). We can possess our purpose by praying into it. Take hold of God's purpose for your life, the life of your family, your community and your church. Declare the goodness of God over you and yours. Declare that no weapon formed against you will be able to prosper. Declare the favor of God for your life, your children, your grandchildren, your community and your church. Don't lay the purposes of God down for your life. Fight the enemy and all his cohorts, so that you will lay hold of God's purpose for your life.

> Don't be passive about the acquiring passion for the Son of God.

One of the new avenues of prayer I was using as we planted a new congregation under the leadership of the Holy Spirit was prayer walking. I would walk through subdivisions, streets of the city, and lay my hands on the doors of all the churches in town, and pray a blessing over them. I was learning to pray Kingdom prayers, not just prayers to bless our new fellowship or prayers that God would cause our fellowship to grow. I was praying prayers of blessing and as I walked, I prayed that we take up the territory for God. God told Joshua, "Every place that the sole of your foot will tread upon I have given you..." (1:3). The Bible says we can pray with purpose in our steps.

† *Release your purpose:* Jesus said, "Now is the judgment of this world; now the ruler of this world will be cast out. And I, if I am lifted up from the earth, will draw all people to Myself" (John 12:31-32). The writer of the book of Proverbs says, "Life and death is in the power of the tongue"(18:21). If we speak negatively over our lives or the lives of others it will produce negative results. If we speak positive, encouraging words it will produce positive, healthy results. I know the power words spoken over you can have on your life and how those words impact you. Our purpose is released through our words and our actions. In fact, our purpose is just waiting to be released though God-given words of promise, hope, encouragement and love that He has for us. Release your future by giving it back to God and asking Him to do with you whatever He desires. John the Baptist stated, "I must decrease and He (Jesus) must increase." Praying with purpose means: to know it, to pray into it, to possess it and to release it.

PRINCIPLE #2 | PRAY WITH PASSION

The second principle of praying in the power of the Spirit is praying with passion. Passionate prayer is "Deep calling unto deep" (Psalm 42:7). Out of the depths of our heart comes a yearning and a cry for the heart to God, for the things of God. Let's look at three ways Hannah cultivated the practice of praying with passion as we find in 1 Samuel 1:8-18. Hannah means *grace* and she was barren, unable to have children. She was disgraced and ridiculed for her barrenness.

One thing we learn about Hannah is she came to the place in her life where she would no longer be passive (vs. 10-11). Dr. Vincent Synan, a prominent church historian observes this about the early Methodist movement, "Our heritage of fiery camp meetings where people flocked to the altars seeking more of God...We were the largest, fastest growing church in the world because of how God moved in those early tent revivals. Ironically, he said that people would come to criticize the Methodist for being too noisy! The meetings led by Rev. John Wesley were characterized by lives being transformed, singing, dancing and weeping and praising

---

Vincent Synan quoted by Terry Teykl, *Pray the Price,* Power Point Press, Muncie, IN, 1997. p. 52-53.

so much that they were impossible to ignore," (*Pray the Price* by Dr. Terry Teykl).

Jack Deere in his book, *Surprised by the Power of the Spirit,* describes passionate prayer, "Don't be passive about acquiring passion for the Son of God. Make it the focus of your life." We had been meeting for nearly nine months together as a small group for fellowship, discipleship, Bible application, with the goal of multiplying. I challenged our small group to take our passionate praying outside into the streets and shared with them the principles of prayer walking. We broke up into groups of twos and threes and set out to pray for the neighborhood. The two ladies in my group were in their late sixties to early seventies. We walked just a short distance to an apartment complex and began praying for the families and individuals living there. We prayed prayers of blessing and declared words of freedom from addictions and other prayers as led by the Holy Spirit. There was a young girl looking frantically around the parking area and as we

> **Many times I have found myself stopping too soon in praying for a situation.**

Jack Deere, *Surprised by the Power of the Spirit,* Zondervan Publishing House, Grand Rapids, MI, p. 201. p.201.

approached, I asked what was the problem. She said, *My vehicle has just been stolen.* We inquired more about it and listened to her story. After a bit we ask, *May we pray with you about your car?* She said, *Sure.* Following the prayer to find her vehicle, one of the older ladies looked up at the young woman and asked, *Do you know Jesus as your personal Savior?* The young lady responded, *No.* My friend asked, *May we pray with you to invite Jesus into your heart?* The young lady replied, *Yes, I would.* Right there in the parking lot, this seventy year old person led us in a prayer as this young lady gave her heart to Jesus. This is praying with passion and obedience to the Holy Spirit.

Another thing we learn about Hannah is that she came to the place in her life where she poured out her heart before the Lord (vs. 12-16). As she was praying passionately her language can best be described in Lamentation 2:19, "Pour out your heart like water before the face of the Lord."

This kind of passionate prayer gets God's attention. Jim Goll in his book *Kneeling on the Promises* observes, "Praying with passion is a language of the heart." Hannah's prayer describes how she poured out

---

Jim Goll, *Kneeling on the Promises,* Chosen Books, Grand Rapids, MI, 1999, p. 61.

her heart before the Lord. "I was pouring out my soul to the Lord...I have been praying here out of my great anguish and grief" (1 Samuel 1:15-16). The Psalmist writes, "Pour out your hearts to Him, for God is our refuge" (62:8).

Passionate prayer takes on these dynamics:

† We become earnest, deep and intense in our prayers. This prayer flows from the depths of the heart.

† We will not be denied access to the heart of God. Jesus likens this kind of praying to, "Ask and keep on asking, knock and keep on knocking, seek and keep on seeking" (Matthew 7:7).

> There is nothing God cannot do with a people who persevere in prayer...

† We desire the heart of God and nothing will satisfy our longing but God alone. "O God, you are my God, earnestly I seek you; my soul thirsts for you..." (Psalm 63:1).

It was in the fall of 1997 when I was having my time of prayer before the Lord, and feeling such an intensity of prayer to come over me that I got on my face before the Lord and began to pray. I don't know if I fell asleep or went into a trance. While in prayer I saw a man's face that I did not recognize. I asked the Lord to show me who that person was but it was not the time for that to be known. A few weeks passed and I was invited to a pastor's gathering and there was a guest evangelist who also joined us. As we went around the table sharing what God was doing in our lives, the picture of the man I saw in my dream came rushing back and I kept looking at this gentlemen to see if that was the man's face. Following lunch together with all the pastors, I asked the visiting evangelist if we could talk.

We went back to the church where the revival services were being held. I began to tell him my story and the vision I had of a man's face. I said to him, "I believe you are the man I saw in that vision." "That is interesting." He replied, "A man came up to him at a place where he had been preaching earlier and said to him, 'There will be a young man who will come up to you and tell you that he saw your face in a vision." I believe in passionate prayer. I believe in pouring our heart out before the Lord. I believe the Lord wants to give us vision of those things yet to come.

For when we have exhausted all our resources and we begin to fix our eyes on Jesus, we find ourselves totally dependent upon the Lord. We have taken our eyes off all the secondary resources and put our eyes upon our primary source, Jesus. We know there is yet more of God to be had and so we storm the heavenlies seeking the Lord with all our heart, mind and strength.

When Hannah began to passionately contend for the purposes of God for her life, she was opening the door of her heart for the Lord to intervene into her circumstances. She was laying hold of the good promises of God and activating His word for her life. She would no longer be driven by shame, embarrassment, ridicule and rejection. She refused to believe the lies of the enemy that she was worthless and beyond help. She was taking her stand. There will be a time in our lives when we get tired of being denied the abundant life God has called us to and has given to us through His Son, Jesus. Our spirit cries out to the Lord, "Enough is enough! I will take my stand and I will stand until my change comes." "All the days of my hard service I will wait, till my change comes" (Job 14:14). Our change will come to those who wait on the Lord—which does not mean inactivity—it simply means we are pressing into the Lord and not giving up or letting go, but taking our stand until God brings about a change in our circumstances or in our lives or in the life of another for whom we are praying.

PRINCIPLE #3 | PRAY WITH PERSEVERANCE

The third principle of prayer that I learned, is how

to pray with perseverance. I don't know about you, but that is not a strong suit of mine. Many times I have found myself stopping too soon in praying for a situation, a person or a breakthrough. Paul writes, "Praying with all prayer and supplication in the Spirit, being watchful to this end with all perseverance and supplication for all the saints" (Ephesians 6:18).

> "No weapon formed against me will be able to prosper."

Someone described perseverance as, "a great oak tree that was simply a small nut but held its ground."

Bob Sorge in his book, *In His Face*, defines perseverance to mean "Steadfast, to endure patiently, to bear up and to wait. The New Testament word for perseverance describes the capacity to bear up under difficult circumstances, not with passive complacency, but with a hopeful fortitude that actively resists weariness and defeat." Webster defines perseverance *"as the steady continued action or belief usually over a long period and especially despite difficulties or setbacks."*

Dick Eastman tells this story, "Much of society has forgotten to persevere...few have a striving spirit like

---

Bob Sorge, *In His Face,* Oasis House, Canandaigua, NY, 1994, p.96-97.

the artist Raphael. Once he was questioned, 'What is your greatest painting?' He smiled, saying, 'My next one.' One finds Raphael always striving to do better. That is what we need in prayer, an attitude of persistence," (*No Easy Road*, 96).

George Muller's nickname was *stayer*. Just to mention one example, "The greatest point is never to give up until the answer comes. I have been praying for sixty-three years and eight months for one man's conversion. He is not saved yet, but he will be. How can it be otherwise...I am praying. The day when Muller's friend received Christ did not come until Muller's casket was lowered in the ground. There near the open grave, this friend gave his heart to God. Prayers of perseverance had won another battle. Muller's success may be summarized in four powerful words: He did not quit." (*No Easy Road*).

The great preacher, Charles Spurgeon said, "By perseverance the snail reached the ark," (Dutch Sheets, *Intercessory Prayer*).

These are days God is calling us to press into Him and not to loosen our grip and not to give up. To give up

---

Dick Eastman. *No Easy Road*, p. 96.

George Muller. *No Easy Road,* p. 97.

Webster Dictionary

now in the face of overwhelming odds and challenging circumstances would give the enemy the victory. We will give no ground to the enemy; we will not give him a place in which to stand, no entrance in which he can sow seeds of doubt, discouragement and defeat. The Apostle Paul states, "Yet in all these things we are more than conquerors through Him who loved us" (Romans 8:37).

There is nothing God cannot do with a people who persevere in prayer, storming the gates of heaven for God to release the rain of His Spirit, for the Lord to give us the breakthroughs we have been praying for, but now is not the time to quit. It is the time to do as Paul describes in his letter to the Ephesians, "Finally, my brethren, be strong in the Lord and in the power of His might...That you may be able to withstand in the evil day, and having done all, to stand" (6:10, 13). Therefore let us ask the Lord to give us the Spirit of perseverance, resolve and determination to pray until our breakthrough comes.

Key verses that encourage us to persevere:
† "Therefore, since we are surrounded by such a great

Charles Spurgeon quoted by Dutch Sheets, *Intercessory Prayer*, Ventura, CA, 1996, p. 17.

cloud of witnesses, let us throw off everything (every discouraging and despairing thought) that hinders and the sin (of unbelief) that so easily entangles, and let us run with perseverance the race marked out for us" (Hebrews 12:1). "You need to persevere so that when you have done the will of God, you will receive what He has promised" (Hebrews 10:36). "But the seed on good soil stands for those with a noble and good heart, who hear the word, retain it, and by perseverance produce a crop" (Luke 8:15).

† Cindy Jacobs in her book *Possessing the Gates of the Enemy* observes the importance of perseverance as Jesus prayed and fasted for forty days while being tempted in the desert by the devil. "The battle was not won in one day. Jesus had spent forty days praying and fasting. We sometimes become discouraged if we have to persevere for one or two days. We must battle for our families, our homes, our loved ones, our community and our church and we don't give up."

† "And let us not lose heart in doing good, for in due time we shall reap if we do not grow weary" (Galatians

---

Cindy Jacobs, *Possessing the Gates of the Enemy*, Chosen Books, Grand Rapids, MI, 1991, p. 232.

6:9).

HOW THEN CAN WE PERSEVERE IN PRAYER?

† When we have *"prayed through"* and have gotten the mind Christ on the matter.
† When we are learning to stand strong in the strength that God provides.
† When we are allowing Christ to transform us to be more like Him.
† When we are keeping our eyes focused on Jesus and not the problems or the challenging circumstances we find ourselves in.
† When we lay aside every weight that drags us down and we run to Him who says, "Come to me all who labor and are heaven laden and I will give you rest, for My yoke is easy and My burden is light" (Matthew 11:28-30).

The Bible describes the wrestling match between Jacob and an Angel. "...Because you have wrestled/struggled with God and with men and have overcome" (Genesis 32:28). What does this convey about the importance of prayer, intercession and making our requests known to God?

† God wants to know how bad we want our answer, our request for which we are praying.

Learning to Pray in the Power of the Spirit

† God wants us to be a bit more violent in our praying. "From the days of John the Baptist until now the Kingdom of heaven suffers violence, and the violent take it by force" (Matthew 11:12). To "take it by force" means, "to press beyond human status quo and religious formalism. It is the result of God's order shaking relationships, households, cities, and nations by the entry of the Holy Spirit's power working in people."

† God wants to teach us about warfare that defeats the enemy and sets the captive free. "For by You I can run against a troop, by my God I can leap over a wall...He teaches my hands to make war" (Psalm 18:29,34).

† Which means I go on the offensive, God will enable me to get over the things I need to get over and I can take hold of the "sword of the Spirit, which is the Word of God" (Ephesians 6:17).

Terry Teykl in his book *Pray the Price* coins the phrase *soaking prayer;* when a person or situation is lifted up before the Lord again and again. He illustrates Frazier Memorial UMC in Montgomery, Alabama has a 24

Teykl, Terry, *Pray the Price,* Power Point Press, Muncie, IN, 1997, p. 33

hour prayer ministry where each request is prayed for several times and filed.

    Their intercessors come and pray over these requests one by one, spending time as the Lord leads them on each. They pray through the box many times in a week. Dr. Teykl explains that "soaking prayer" is "persevering prayer. Jesus said, 'And will not God vindicate His elect who cry out to Him day and night?' (Luke 18:7). Jesus was equating faith with perseverance. I believe that sometimes it takes persistent almost stubborn prayer to reach a spiritual breakthrough because even though God is eager to answer the prayers of His people, sometimes there may be factors in a situation that we simply do not see."

Could this be our prayer of perseverance?

    Lord, I come to you in the strong name of Jesus, standing in His strength to stay the course and to press into You and to Your purpose. Lord, I ask that You give me the faith to hold on like that of a bulldog – to pray and not to let go until I have a breakthrough (name what thing or area in which you are needing a breakthrough). Lord, I ask that You would help me not just to hold on, but really see Your hand at work (name that area or situation in which you need to see the Lord's handiwork and the display of His glory). Make this declaration with me. "No weapon formed against me (by the enemy) will be able to prosper" (Isaiah 54:17). Declare: "That greater is He who is in me than he who is in the world" (1 John 4:4). Learn to pray with perseverance!

PRINCIPLE #4 | PRAYING WITH POWER

The fourth principle I learned is that we can pray with power as modeled by the disciples, recorded in Acts 4:23-33.

Let's examine this model in three ways:

† *Praying with power is to pray in agreement.* The disciples, "...raised their voice in one accord" (Acts 4:24). In the midst of this intimidating mandate by the religious community not to speak, teach or carry on the ministry of Jesus they said, "Whether it is right in the sight of God, you judge. For we cannot but speak the things which we have seen and heard" (Acts 4:19-20). The Apostle Paul writes, "Now I plead with you, brethren, by the name of our Lord Jesus Christ, that you all speak the same thing..." (1 Corinthians 1:10). That is "having a uniform testimony." "Again I say to you that if two of you agree on earth concerning anything that they ask, it will be done for them by my Father in heaven" (Matt. 18:19).

† *Praying with power is the activation of the name of Jesus.* "By stretching out Your hand to heal and that signs and wonders may be done through the name of Your holy Servant Jesus" (Acts 4:30).
  - The Apostle Paul states, "Therefore God also has highly exalted Him and given Him the name which is above every name, that at the name of Jesus every knee should bow, of those in heaven, and of those on earth, and of those under the earth, and that every tongue should confess that Jesus Christ is Lord, to the glory of God the Father" (Philippians 2:9-11).
  - The Psalmist declared, "O Lord, our Lord, how excellent is Your name in all the earth, who have set Your glory about the heavens" (8:1).
  - Why activate the name of Jesus?
    † There is *power* in His name.
    † There is *provision* in His name.
    † There is *pardon* in His name.
    † There is *pleasure* in His name. "You will show me the path of life; in Your presence is fullness of joy; at Your right hand are pleasures forevermore" (Psalm 16:11).
† *Praying with power is being filled with the Holy Spirit.* "And when they had prayed, the place where they

were assembled together was shaken; and they were all filled with the Holy Spirit, and they spoke the word of God with boldness" (Acts 4:31).

- o The Bible declares that signs would follow those who believe. Signs of peace, joy, healing, freedom, signs of unity, agreement, love, grace and mercy and the manifest presence of His power would be displayed before mankind. Jesus said, "Behold, I send the Promise of My Father upon you; but tarry in the city of Jerusalem until you are endued with power from on high" (Luke 24:49).

† This last principle of praying with power is to *know who we are in Christ Jesus.* "And with great power the apostles gave witness to the resurrection of the Lord Jesus. And great grace was upon them all"(Acts 4:33).

Let us boldly declare: The ability to pray with power is to know that I am a child of God, that I have been birthed into the Kingdom of God. I know that I am an heir of God and a joint-heir of Jesus Christ. I know that my position is not because of my goodness, but because of Christ's righteousness in me. I can pray with power not because of my name, but in the name of the One to whom I belong. I can invoke His name and know

His presence, His power, His provision, His pardon and His pleasure.

May God's rich blessings be poured upon you as you live the Spirit-filled life. I invite you to engage yourself and others, and apply the truths and principles found in the study guide section titled, *Pray in the Power of the Spirit,* found in the back of the book (p.253-265).

Chapter 7
JESUS - THE ULTIMATE MODEL OF SPIRIT-FILLED LIVING

We began our journey in my desperate attempt to find purpose and meaning in life. When I experienced the unconditional love and acceptance of Jesus Christ. As I listened to the witnesses sharing their stories of the transformation Jesus had made in their lives at our Lay Witness Mission. We moved along in our journey as we experienced the baptism of the Holy Spirit while attending Camp Farthest Out and discovered the fire of God's Spirit He imparts as evidence of His presence and power. A fire to seek His face, a fire to share His love and our faith, and a fire that cleanses and makes whole. Through the years of serving the Lord, whether through pastoral leadership or in some other capacity of service and ministry, I have discovered the absolute necessity of seeking Jesus, looking to Jesus and allowing His life to be lived through us. We look to Jesus because He is our model of service and ministry. He is our model of total dependence upon our heavenly Father. Jesus said, "Most assuredly, I say to you, the Son can do nothing of Himself" (John 5:19). He is our model to live by, as Paul addresses the Athenians, "For in Him, [Jesus], we live and move and have our being" (Acts 17:28). For apart from Him we can do nothing (John 15:5) and He intends for us to understand that. Leonard Sweet and Frank Viola make this observation, "But Christ is the gravitational pull that brings everything together and gives it meaning. Without Him, all things lose their value." This is the reason the writer of Hebrews exhorts us to, "Look unto Jesus the Author and Finisher of our faith..." (12:2). The word "look" signifies undivided attention, looking away from all distractions in order to fix one's gaze on one object. We

---

Leonard Sweet and Frank Viola, *Jesus Manifesto*, Thomas Nelson, Nashville, TN, 2010, p. xv Introduction and p.21

Spirit-Filled Life Bible, Thomas Nelson Publishers, Nashville, TN 1991, p. 1887.

Jesus – the Ultimate Model of Spirit-filled Living

journey through this life beholding Jesus, looking to Jesus, gazing upon His beauty. As Helen H. Lemmel declares in the precious words from her song "Turn Your Eyes Upon Jesus," once our eyes are opened to see the incredible richness and captivating beauty of Jesus, either our pursuits will take a backseat, or we will discover them anew and afresh "...in the light of His glory and grace."

Jesus' ministry was launched following his baptism in the Jordan by John the Baptist. This is his testimony as Matthew in his Gospel describes, "When He had been baptized. Jesus came up immediately from the water; and behold, the heavens were opened to Him, and he saw the Spirit of God descending like a dove and alighting upon Him. And suddenly a voice came from heaven, saying, 'This is My beloved Son, in whom I am well pleased'" (3:16-17). Followed by this baptismal experience, Jesus was led by the Spirit into the wilderness and tempted by the devil for forty days (Luke 4:1-2a). Jesus exited the wilderness experience successfully combating the enemy through the word of God and the power of the Spirit, "Then Jesus returned in the power of the Spirit to Galilee, and news of Him went out though all the surrounding region" (Luke 4:14). Finally, Jesus describes His ministry this way, "The

Spirit of the Lord is upon Me, because He has anointed me to preach the gospel to the poor; He has sent Me to heal the brokenhearted, to proclaim liberty to the captives and recovery of sight to the blind, to set at liberty those who are oppressed; to proclaim the acceptable year of the Lord" (Luke 4:18-19).

If we are looking to imitate Jesus, if we are seeking to emulate Him, and for Him to live His life through us, then our only conclusion is: we too need our baptism of the Spirit. Though Jesus never sinned, He gave us an example to follow. We need His baptism of the Holy Spirit. As John the Baptist explains, "He will baptize you with the Holy Spirit and fire" (Luke 3:16). We know that we will encounter spiritual warfare as Paul admonishes, "Put on the whole armor of God, that you may be able to stand against the wiles (schemes) of the devil" (Ephesians 6:11). We also know that the Spirit of Jesus must increase in our life, as John the Baptist declared, "He must increase, but I must decrease" (John 3:30). Finally, we too will be launched into ministry and service for it the same as Jesus, "To preach to the poor, to heal the brokenhearted, proclaim liberty to the captives and recovery of sight to the blind, to set at

Jesus – the Ultimate Model of Spirit-filled Living

liberty the oppressed and to proclaim the presence of the Lord in the midst of us is mighty" (Luke 4:18-19). Jesus said, "He who believes in Me, the works that I do he will do also; and greater works than these He will do; because I go to the Father" (John 14:12). Jesus is our model, we do look to Him and we desire to receive all that He has to give us.

Let's examine *four aspects* on how Jesus is our model of Spirit-filled living. Our prayer is not just to be like Jesus, but we are so surrendered to His Lordship that Jesus has direct access to every area of our lives and is able to live His life through us. As we begin this lesson together will you pray with me:

> **Jesus is our model, we do look to Him and we desire to receive all that He has to give us.**

> *Come Lord Jesus, and live through me, let me think your thoughts, let me feel what you feel, let me see through your eyes, let me be so attached to you that those things of lasting value will remain and bear fruit that honors and glorifies your name. Amen!*

EXAMINING FOUR ASPECTS ON HOW JESUS IS OUR MODEL OF SPIRIT-FILLED LIVING

ASPECT #1 |

The first aspect of the ministry Jesus modeled before us was His prayer life. The disciples had been observing the priority that prayer had for Jesus. They were observing the intensity in which He prayed and observing the results of His prayer life, and came to Jesus inquiring, "Lord, teach us to pray" (Luke 11:1). Prayer does not come naturally, but supernaturally; for prayer originates with God and we simply pray back to Him what He has placed upon our hearts to pray. The Lord teaches us to pray when we come to the conclusion we don't really know how to pray as we ought, but we seek the Spirit's help to pray those things that God has place upon our hearts to pray. "Likewise the Spirit helps in our weakness. For we do not know what we should pray for as we ought, but the Spirit Himself makes intercession for us with groanings which cannot be uttered" (Romans 8:26). Coming to the conclusion we need someone beyond ourselves to teach us how to pray means we have come to a place of humility. We have a teachable spirit, likened to what the Psalmist explains, "Teach me your way, O Lord; I will walk in your truth" (86:11).

Jesus – the Ultimate Model of Spirit-filled Living

I have discovered three truths about learning how to pray:

First, learn to pray the word of God. There is not a better prayer that can be prayed than the inspired word of God. One of the great joys and insights into Scripture is to pray back God's word to Himself. For example, I will take the apostolic prayers of Paul's letters to the churches and turn them into prayer and personalize them as found in Colossians 1:10-14. "Father, I ask that I may walk worthy of the Lord, to fully please Him in every thing I say and do, that You would cause me to be fruitful in every good work and to increase in knowing You. Father, I ask that You would strengthen me with Your might, through Your glorious power of Your Spirit and to be patient in all things as I am being filled with joy that comes from knowing You as my heavenly Father. Father, I give thanks to you for qualifying me to take part in Your Kingdom and to enjoy the inheritance I have in being a part Your family. Father, thank You for delivering me from the power of darkness and transferring me into the Kingdom of Your beloved Son, Jesus. For You have redeemed me through the cleansing blood of Christ and I receive His forgiveness for all my sins."

Create your own prayers to the Father as you pray back to Him His very own word. I believe the disciples saw the intimacy Jesus had with His heavenly Father and inquired, "How may we have that same intimacy?"

Second, I have learned to make prayer personal, powerful and practical. Wait upon the Lord and listen with intention for His voice and pray those words and phrases that flow from the Father's heart. I remind the Lord of His word. The Psalmist declared, "Rest in the Lord and wait patiently for Him..." (37:7). Waiting before the Lord is such a powerful act. Claudio Freidzon in his book, *Holy Spirit I Hunger For You*, observes these truths about waiting. First, "Waiting indicates that God has priority." That is, I don't go rushing in and rushing out of His presence. I take time to listen, to be awestruck at His beauty and to be refreshed in His presence, "I waited patiently for the Lord; he turned to me and heard my cry" (Psalm 40:1). Second, "Waiting allows God to work in us and weaken our wills, so that we will give in to His will." Waiting gives the Lord opportunity to purify our desires, our motives and our purpose. Waiting allows the Lord time to prepare us and prepare the place or the

---

Claudio Freidzon, *Holy Spirit I Hunger For You,* Creation House, Lake Mary, FL, 1997, p. 149.

Jesus – the Ultimate Model of Spirit-filled Living

people to which He is sending us. The writer of Hebrews picks up on the prophetic words of the Psalmist as he speaks of the ministry of Jesus, "Then I said, 'Behold, I have come – in the volume of the book it is written of Me – To do Your will, O God'" (Hebrews 10:7).

Third, waiting indicates the "seriousness of our request." If we really desire something we will be willing to wait for it to come to fruition. We will resist the notion to try and make something happen. We will wait upon the Lord and get our assignment from Him, because the Father knows best!

I learned this practice of waiting before the Lord in a devotional way while in college. I had been reading a book by Andrew Murray entitled, *Waiting Upon God.* I began practicing the truths and principles he shared about waiting upon God. This principle was reinforced by Mark Virkler in his book, *Listening to God.* I learned to journal the thoughts that flowed from the heart of the Father. I would usually begin this prayer time by asking the Lord a question, listening for His response, recording those thoughts and praying them back to God. Again, this is a time of getting quiet before the Lord, waiting upon Him and listening for that still small voice of the Holy Spirit. It is practicing what the Psalmist instructs, "Be still, and know that I am God…" (46:10). These are the ingredients the disciples saw in Jesus and inquired how they, too, could pray the way Jesus did. The thing that got the disciples attention was His prayer life.

ASPECT #2 |

The second aspect about Jesus being our spiritual model is His commitment to make disciples. Jesus took very seriously the gathering of disciples around him. They were far from perfect, but they carried within themselves great possibilities. They were not selected because they were the most "likely to succeed." They were not selected on the basis of their charismatic personality. They were not selected for their cool demeanor, or their ability to articulate certain creeds or doctrines. They were just ordinary men, selected not at random, but very intentionally. "Now it came to pass in those days that He went out to the mountain to pray, and continued all night in prayer to God. And when it was day, He called His disciples to Himself, and from them He chose twelve whom He also called apostles" (Luke 6:12-13). We see very clearly that selecting and making disciples is very intentional and Jesus demonstrated it all begins with prayer.

While attending Oral Roberts University, Tom Albin asked Bob Braman and me to meet with him for

Jesus – the Ultimate Model of Spirit-filled Living

Bible study, prayer and accountability for an entire year. I will say that was one of the most important years of my spiritual development. Since that time I have sought to replicate that model of meeting with a few others for Bible study, prayer and accountability. I discovered you can start this with those who are not yet Christians. At the first church I served out of seminary in Johnson City, Tennessee I asked two men to meet for Bible study and prayer. Neither of these had made a commitment to Jesus Christ. A few weeks into our meeting together I asked them if they would like to invite Jesus into their hearts and both affirmed they would like to do so. I believe by following our Head, Jesus, our main calling and responsibility is to make disciples.

> ...by following our Head, Jesus, our main calling and responsibility is to make disciples.

Bill Hull in his book *The Disciple-Making Pastor* observes, "Disciple making should be installed at the heart of the church, and the commanded product of the church is a fruit-bearing believer called a discipleship."

Bill Hull, *The Disciple-Making Pastor,* Fleming H. Revell, Grand Rapid, MI, 1988, p. 50.

Journey in Discipleship

So the question remains: Why did Jesus choose such a model for us to follow? What can we learn from His method of making disciples? Why is the church so reluctant to make disciples? What would it look like if we took seriously an intentional plan for making disciples? To answer these questions would be quite lengthy, but let me suggest a few brief thoughts. Jesus chose this model because it can be readily *duplicated*. Jesus used this method because it leads to *transformed* lives. Jesus knew churches would have to make a *decision* if they were going to make members or make disciples. Most churches opted for making members instead of making disciples because to make disciples means there is an expectation to grow and mature in their walk with Christ. Finally, Jesus knew that if we took disciple making seriously it would result in the *transformation* of the world. Jesus also knew that it would only happen if an intentional approach to making disciples was in place.

George Barna in his book *Growing True Disciples* clarifies what discipleship is about, "We might define discipleship as becoming a complete and competent follower of Jesus Christ. It is about the intentional

---

George Barna, *Growing True Disciples,* Water Brook Press, Colorado Springs, CO, 2001, p17.

Jesus – the Ultimate Model of Spirit-filled Living

training of people who voluntarily submit to the lordship of Christ and who want to become imitators in every thought, word, and deed."

Jesus knew that discipleship grew out of relationships, not out of programs. Discipleship can never become one of the programs in the church and have any lasting value or fruit. Authentic discipleship grows out of relationship and that is the reason Jesus called His disciples, *"friends"* not *"servants"* (John 15:15).

> Jesus knew that discipleship grew out of relationships...

Joel Comiskey's book, *The Relational Discipleship*, draws upon Thomas Hawkins' observation concerning the Wesleyan movement, "John Wesley recognized the fundamental connection between discipleship and community. Many other preachers of the English revival engaged in field preaching. Wesley alone organized his followers into small communities that provided a tool kit of practices and a network of companions. Early Methodists discovered that mutual accountability within

---

Joel Comiskey, *The Relational Discipleship*, CCS Publishing, Moreno Valley, CA, 2010, p. 115.

a spiritual community effectively built up a consistent discipleship."

Discipleship takes place when we see people through the eyes of Jesus, asking Him to show you who He wants you to pour your life out into, asking Him to send you those who are hungry to go on with the Lord or those who just need some encouragement to move on past where they are in their walk with Christ. Paul's letter to Timothy instructs him to do this in his disciple making strategy, "And the things you have heard from among many witnesses, commit these to faithful men who will be able to teach others also" (2 Timothy 2:2). Making disciples is not rocket science, but it does take lots of commitment. It takes a plan on moving folks along in their walk with Christ. It takes plenty of prayer to see that person mature in Christ and for you to maintain a continual feeding upon God's word and staying refreshed in His Spirit. It may not be rocket science, but it takes the same boldness and courage to step out and gather two or three people together for Bible study, prayer and accountability. In closing, authentic discipleship takes place when a disciple can become a disciple-maker.

Aspect #3 |

The third aspect about Jesus being our spiritual model is His compassion. Jesus saw the multitude and was "moved with compassion, because they were weary and scattered" (Matthew 9:36). Jesus saw the sick and "He was moved with compassion for them and healed their sick" (Matthew 14:14). The writer of Lamentations states this about the Lord's compassion, "Through the Lord's mercies we are not consumed, because His compassions fail not" (3:22). This means that Jesus was deeply moved by the people's lack of spiritual leadership and their need for healing and wholeness.

These verses tell us this about our Lord's compassion:

† *We become weary and need His strength.*
† *We become scattered (we lose our way) and need His leading.*
† *We become sick (emotionally, physically or spiritually) and need His healing touch.*

Peter and John were on their way to the temple to pray and a man was begging for assistance for his daily need for food. Peter and John stopped and looked at him and said, "Silver and gold I do not have in the name of

Jesus Christ of Nazareth, rise up and walk" (Acts 3:6). The crippled man (who had been this way from birth) responded to those life giving words and hope filled his heart. Faith infused his spirit and he stood to his feet "walking leaping and praising God" (Acts 3:8). One of the important steps in this man getting up on his feet was that Peter reached out his hand and "lifted him up" (Acts 3:7). We find three important ingredients to this man's healing through the compassionate acts of Peter and John. Remember Jesus said, "The works I do you shall do also..." (John 14:12). Jesus had compassion upon the lame, the blind, the leper, the demonized and those who had died and needed a resurrection. Jesus touched them, felt what they felt and brought healing, release and freedom to their lives. The disciples with Jesus now living in the power of the Holy Spirit, were able to share in the Lord's compassion for others. We find in showing compassion we have encouraging words to share with others. We carry within us the words of life, liberty, freedom and wholeness. We can declare the Good News of the Gospel to those who need to hear it. Jesus said, "The words that I speak to you are spirit, and they are life" (John 6:63). Peter spoke words of life to this crippled man. The second way we find Peter and John showed compassion of Christ was that they stopped and listened to this man. One of the most compassionate things we can do is to stop and listen to the story of someone who may be experiencing pain, hurt, or loss and needs someone to hear their cry for help. Peter and John stopped and took time before they worshiped to hear the cry of humanity just outside the church, waiting for someone to address the deeper need in his life.

The last act of compassion Peter and John showed was to reach out their hand and give this man the lift he needed. It is one thing to speak words of life and to listen with a caring ear. Yet to stretch out your hand and take them by the hand and practically help them up can be vital. Some folks just need someone to reach out and take them by the hand and give them the lift in life they need. Peter and John were demonstrating the heart and life of Jesus as they showed compassion to the man, who has now become a worshiper with them, "So he, leaping up, stood and walked and entered the temple with them – walking, leaping and praising God" (Acts 3:8). There are many outside the church waiting for the healing words of Christ to be spoken over them, to know someone cares by taking time and listening to their story and giving them a hand to see the transformational work of the Holy Spirit. This is what happened: the man changed his focus as Peter and John said, "Look at us..." (Acts 3:4), Peter and John demonstrated compassion of Jesus, "What I do have I give to you..." (Acts 3:6) and a changed life opened the door for the Good News of the Gospel to be received, "...many of those who heard the word believed; and the number of the men were about five thousand..." (Acts 4:4). One changed life can impact the masses. The reason we can show and demonstrate compassion is because we are recipients of the compassion of Jesus as he said, "Freely you have received, freely give" (Matthew 10:8).

We find yet another beautiful encounter of the compassion of Jesus shown toward a man who needed to go a bit higher in order to get a glimpse of Jesus. And Zacchaeus sought to see who Jesus was, but could not because of the crowd, "For he was of short stature. So he ran ahead and climbed up into a sycamore tree to see Him, for He was going to pass that way" (Luke 19:3-4). What was it that drove Zaccheaus to do such a desperate thing? He had a deep desire to see who Jesus was, "And He sought to see who Jesus was..." (v.3). He was a man who expressed a courageous faith, "And he climbed up into a sycamore tree" (v. 4). He was a man who felt a deep emptiness in his life, that desperately needed to be filled and this is what Jesus saw when He passed by. Zacchaeus discovered while out on the limb that he could release the past so that he could embrace the future. Jesus offered to Zacchaeus compassion and grace as He said, "Zaccheaus, make haste and come down, for today I must stay at your house" (v. 5). Jesus came that we might enjoy His forgiveness, that we might enter into a vital relationship with Him and that we might encounter His transforming power working in our lives so that we can release our past to the Lord and embrace the future He has for us. Zaccheaus discovered the love of God while out on the limb, "...today salvation has come to this house" (v. 9). Zaccheaus discovered that friendship with God is not based on performance. Jesus wanted to be his friend before a life change took place. Zaccheaus discovered God's unconditional love and acceptance and he discovered that "...love covers a multitude of sins" (James 5:20). Finally, Zaccheaus discovered the Lord's purpose for his life while out on a limb, "For the Son of Man has come to seek and to save that which was lost" (Luke 19:10). The Lord wants to show us that same kind of compassion which He showed toward the lame man, and toward those who needed

Christ's unconditional love and acceptance. Have you gone out on a limb lately? It is the place where we encounter the presence of Christ. It is the place where we experience the power of Christ. It is the place where we enjoy the provision of Christ to heal, release and forgive. And, it is the place where we embrace the promise of Christ.

ASPECT #4 |

The fourth aspect about Jesus being our spiritual model is His servant's heart. Jesus rose from the table, "And laid aside His garments, took a towel and girded Him...and He began to wash the disciples' feet" (John 13:4-5). Jesus said, "If anyone serves Me, let him follow Me; and where I am, there My servant will be also..." (John 12:26). The phrase "...and laid aside..." reminds us of Paul's description of Jesus, "Let this mind be in you which was also in Christ Jesus, who, being in the form of God, did not consider it robbery to be equal with God, but made Himself of no reputation taking the form of a bond-servant, and coming in the likeness of men. And being found in appearance as a man, He humbled Himself and became obedient to the point of death, even the death of the cross" (Philippians 2:5-8).

Jesus – the Ultimate Model of Spirit-filled Living

Jesus is our example for gaining a servant's heart as He said, "For I have given you an example, that you should do as I have done to you" (John 13:15). What was the act of servanthood Jesus showed toward his disciples? "He poured water into a basin and began to wash the disciples' feet, and to wipe them with the towel with which He was girded" (John 13:5). Though this may not have been a very pleasant task, Jesus chose to serve the disciples by washing their feet. For up to that point, no one had stepped forward to wash the disciples' feet. There are times, and there are places Jesus calls us to serve, though the task is quite unpleasant. There are assignments that God gives to us and He simply asks us to be obedient, knowing full well He is working His character into our lives. Sometimes it is not the assignment that counts, but the deeper thing God is doing in our hearts. Jesus began to wash the disciples' feet and His ministry of washing feet became misunderstood. "Then He came to Simon Peter. And Peter said to Him, 'Lord, are You washing my feet?'" (John 13:6). There are times when we do not want the touch of Jesus upon our lives. We feel so exposed and vulnerable that it makes us very uncomfortable and we almost pull away, because we do not understand what Jesus is doing.

Jesus is saying a couple of things as He washed Peter's feet. First, we must welcome Christ's touch upon every area of our life, no matter how uncomfortable it might be for the moment. Second, there will be those who will resist our desire to serve and we will be misunderstood by others. Yet, we must press through so that God's work in our lives can go forward. Jesus said, "What I am doing you do not understand now, but you will know after this" (John 13:7). We serve and give and we leave the results up to the Holy Spirit to give insight and understanding to what God is doing through our lives and in our lives. Developing a servant's heart allows for several things to happen. First, it gives way to Christ's Lordship in our lives, "If I then, your Lord and Teacher, have washed your feet, you also ought to wash one another's feet" (John 13:14). Second, we do as the One upon whom our eyes are fixed, "Most assuredly, I say to you, a servant is not greater than his master..." (John 13:16). Jesus is our example, we follow Him and we are not above our Lord. We can't pick and choose where or how we serve, we just serve out of love and devotion and obedience to Jesus Christ. We do not follow Jesus in words only, but also in our doing. "If you know these things, blessed are you if you do them" (John 13:17). Developing a servant's heart flows out of the new commandment Jesus gives to us, "A new commandment I give to you, that you love one another; as I have loved you, that you also love one another. By this all will know that you are My disciples, if you have love for one another" (John 13:34-35). This is why and how we are to serve one another and have the heart of Jesus living in us and through us.

Jesus is our spiritual model. The only way we can model the life of Jesus is by Jesus living His life through us. This happens as we become fully devoted followers of Jesus opening our lives to Him, giving Jesus full access to our lives, making ourselves available to Him.

Jesus is the ultimate model of Spirit-filled living. Through His prayer life, by the method He used in making disciples, to how He showed and demonstrated compassion, to how He modeled a servant's heart, we fix our eyes on Jesus, the Author and Finisher of our faith.

We look to Jesus because:

† His life, death and resurrection. We see His healing touch upon the lame, the blind and the forsaken. We see His mercy and grace toward those who were in bondage to sin to set the captive free. We see the servant heart of Jesus in seeking the lost, the lonely and the forgotten.

† We want to be like Him. For we too, desire to touch others with the Love of Christ. We, too, desire to see the captive set free. We too desire to be dispensers of God's mercy and grace. We, too, desire to have the servant heart of Jesus.

† He is not just as an example to try and follow; Jesus modeled how to be about ministry and service. He modeled how to make disciples. Jesus knew when He said "Follow Me," He was saying, "Follow Me as I follow My Heavenly Father." The only way to live like Jesus, follow Jesus and model Jesus – is to have Jesus living His life through us.

May God's rich blessings be poured upon you as you live the Spirit-filled life. I invite you to engage yourself and others, and apply the truths and principles found in the study guide section titled, *Jesus – the ultimate model of Spirit-filled living,* found in the back of the book (p.267-278).

Epilogue

Thank you for journeying with me through living the Spirit-filled life. I hope you have been both encouraged and inspired that God can take us where we are and take us to where He wants us to be. I hope you have taken the time to work through the lessons at the end of the book, for reflection and application of the truths and principles we have uncovered in our journey.

I believe the truths and principles found in this book cannot be practiced and implemented into our lives apart from connecting with others to journey with. I believe it is in Christian community that the truths and principles come alive and find expression. Howard Snyder in his book *The Problem of Wine Skins* explains, "It is my conviction that the Koinonia, [fellowship] of the

---

Snyder, Howard A. *The Problem of Wine Skins,* Intervarsity Press, Dowers Grove, IL, p.98.

Holy Spirit is most likely to be experienced when Christians meet together informally in small-group fellowship." Living the Spirit-filled life cannot be done in isolation and God never intended it to be that way. We need to be connected to Jesus Christ and we need to be connected to others, for us to find expression to living a fruitful life. Apart from Christ we can do nothing of lasting value. Being connected to others assists us to build those things of value into our lives. It is in the community of believers that we discover and fulfill our purpose in Christ and through His church. We need the Christian community so that we can navigate life through their counsel, prayers and support. We need the encouragement of Scripture that God's word is a light to our path and lamp to our feet, when we need His direction. We need to connect with the Christian community with like-minded people who are going in the same direction we are going in. We need the Christian community that holds the same values, principles and vision to be aware those who are not yet Christians come to know Christ and be filled with His Holy Spirit. We need Jesus who not only has given us a model to follow, but we need Christ living in us, *The Hope of glory.* We need more than just to see the model fleshed out in Jerusalem, Galilee and Nazareth. We need Christ filling

EPILOGUE

every fiber in our bodies with Himself. We want to know Him personally, intimately and passionately; to live with the Savior, whom we love, because He first loved us.

My encouragement is that you journey through the lessons for study and application at the end of this book. We also encourage you to gather with a few others to go through the study guide together and the questions for group study. You will find it to be not only a time of personal reflection, but corporate reflection.

My prayer is that you will allow Christ to fill you completely with Himself and for Him to be the satisfaction of who you are and find in Him all that you need and even more.

The Study Guide

First of all, make sure all participants have the weekly lessons to be completed throughout the week so that when they come together for discussion and application, they will know what the topic is for that week, thus leading to a more productive discussion. They will have already been reflecting on the truths and principles of that lesson, so that they will be ready to receive additional information at the weekly gathering.

The Spirit-Filled Life lessons can be done with a group of people from three to twelve participants over a seven week period. Jesus said that where two or three are gathered in His name, there He is in the midst of them (Matthew 18:20). Jesus worked with a group of disciples from three to twelve men. The number of participants is not as important as the commitment of the participants to grow in discipleship, become fully devoted followers of Jesus Christ and to walk in the fullness of the Spirit.

The suggestion is that the groups meet outside the church walls, but if there are no other places in which to meet, then use a small classroom in the church for your study. The closer the proximity of the participants to one another, the more the group dynamics increase. It is also a good idea to form a circle so that the participants can see one another and have greater dialogue; and so that when the prayer time comes, you will be able to circle up to pray for one another and any other needs that might be expressed.

The Spirit-Filled Life lessons are not an end in itself, but a means of producing more and better disciples. It is a means of increasing and empowering others for service, ministry and leadership. The Spirit-Filled Life lessons are a method of catching a vision to become disciple-makers. The very goal of the Spirit-Filled Life lessons is to produce fully devoted followers of Jesus Christ, to be empowered by the Holy Spirit to make

THE STUDY GUIDE

disciples, to meet together for fellowship, and to reach out to others with the goal of multiplication.

The Spirit-Filled Life lessons are filled with Scriptural references, principles and truths that will touch our hearts; encourage our spirit and fill us with a sense of hope and promise. The Spirit-Filled Life lessons are a tool to assist us in our journey as disciples of Jesus Christ, be conformed to His image, and to grow from "strength to strength" and from "grace to grace" and from "faith to faith."

Our hope and prayer is that God would fill you with His Spirit as you receive all that He desires to give you and that you will be equipped and empowered by His Spirit for effective service and ministry in and through the name of Jesus Christ.

Grace to you.

Lesson 1

HOW CAN WE LIVE A SPIRIT-FILLED LIFE?

Sports writers and analysts describe how football or basketball games change from high school to college. The game moves faster. Then moving from college to pro the game excels to yet a greater speed. The players will respond by stepping up their game.

Spiritual living is going from "faith to faith" (Romans 1:17), from "grace to grace" (John 1:14) and from "glory to glory" (2 Corinthians 3:17).

Objective | Spiritual living is devoting oneself to knowing Jesus Christ and the transforming power of the Holy Spirit. Spiritual living means knowing who we are in Christ Jesus. Spiritual living is growing and maturing in Christ and seeking to live obedient to Him.

LET'S LOOK AT FOUR KEYS TO SPIRITUAL LIVING

A. First of all, spiritual living displays the posture of our heart: "And you became followers of us and of the Lord, having received the word in much affliction, with joy of the Holy Spirit, so that you became examples to all in Macedonia and Achaia who believe. For from you the word of the Lord came forth...your faith toward God has gone out, so that we do not need to say anything" (1 Thessalonians 1:6-8).

The posture of the heart described by Peter in his Epistle is "to be clothed with humility...but God gives grace to the humble" (1 Peter 5:5).

Spiritual living is taking on the heart of Christ. "Let this mind be in you which was also in Christ Jesus...He humbled Himself and became obedient to the point of death, even death of the cross" (Philippians 2:5, 8).

† According to 1 Thessalonians 1:6-8 how did the church receive and respond to the preaching of the Gospel by the Apostle Paul? What effect did it have upon their lives?

_____
_____
_____
_____

† Describe the kind of attitude we are to have as stated in Philippians 2:5, 8 and what does God give to those who cultivate that kind of attitude according to 1 Peter 5:5?

_____

_____

_____

_____

B. Second, spiritual living examines the position of the heart. The position of the heart is that we take on the heart of a servant. "But he who is greatest among you shall be your servant. And whoever exalts himself will be humbled, and he who humbles himself will be exalted" (Matthew 23:11-12).

The position of the heart is not so much about service, ministry, position or opportunity. It is about faithfulness, character and integrity - placing one's self under the mighty hand of God no matter what instrument He uses.

- It may be serving under someone less talented or gifted.

- It may be serving the Lord and we are being hidden away.
- The Lord goes by calling, integrity, faithfulness and character, not by talent, ability or opportunity.

Before God releases vision, He first deals with our character, because if we are not living with integrity, honesty and with godly character, we will not be able to carry His vision. He deals first with the person, before He entrusts him with His vision.

† What happens to those who refuse to walk in humility?

_____

_____

_____

_____

† What results from walking with a humble and contrite heart?

_____

_____

† Describe why you think God honors faithfulness, character and integrity over service, ministry, position and opportunity?

___

___

___

C. Third, spiritual living describes the purpose of my heart. "But He knows the way that I take; when He has tested me, I shall come forth as gold. My foot has held fast to His steps; I have kept His way and not turned aside. I have not departed from the commandment of His lips; I have treasured the words of His mouth more than my necessary food" (Job 23:10-12).

† What is the purpose of testing?

___

___

___

† What is our response to be toward testing?

___

___

† What connection does Job make between testing and treasuring God's word?

_____

_____

_____

D. Finally, spiritual living means that we are tapping into the promises of God. "But may the God of all grace, who called us to His eternal glory by Christ Jesus, after you have suffered a while, perfect, establish, strengthen, and settle you," (1 Peter 5:10).
   1. He will *perfect* you. The word "perfect" means to restore, to mend, to repair. The Lord restores what sin has taken, He will mend what sin has broken and He will complete what is lacking "will not lack for any good thing" (Psalm 34:10).
   2. He will *establish* you. It means to go resolutely in a certain direction, to be steadfast. "Now to Him who is able to establish you" (Romans 16:25).
   3. He will *strengthen* you. It means to give vigor or to make firm. "I can do all things through Christ who strengthens me" (Philippians 3:16).
   4. He will *settle* you. It means to consolidate or to lay a foundation. God will consolidate all the

fragments of our lives so that we can lay a solid foundation.

† Which one of these describes your life now?

___

† Which one of these describes the prayer you have for your life?

___

† What do you think it would take for that prayer to come to fruition?

___

Spiritual living affects the posture of our heart, describes the position of our heart toward God, so that we embrace the purpose of God and so activates His promises for our lives.

WESLEY'S COVENANT PRAYER

I am no longer my own, but thine.
Put me to what thou wilt, rank me with whom thou wilt.
Put me to doing, put me to suffering.
Let me be employed for thee or laid aside for thee,
exalted for thee or brought low for thee.
Let me be full, let me be empty.
Let me have all things, let me have nothing.
I freely and heartily yield all things to thy pleasure and disposal.
And now, O glorious and blessed God, Father, Son and Holy Spirit,
thou art mine, and I am thine. So be it.
And the covenant which I have made on earth,
let it be ratified in heaven.
Amen.

John Wesley

REFLECTION QUESTIONS

1. Describe one thing you learned from this lesson.

   _____

   _____

   _____

   _____

2. What challenged you the most about this lesson?

   _____

   _____

   _____

   _____

3. Do you have a greater understanding about spiritual living and in what way will it affect your life?

   _____

   _____

   _____

   _____

Journey in Discipleship

MATCHING

I. *(Match the number with the Scripture)*

1. "When He has tested me..."
2. "So that you became examples..."
3. "He who humbles himself will be exalted..."
4. "Perfect, establish, strengthen and settle you..."

___ 1 Peter 5:10

___ Matthew 23:11-12

___ Job 23:10-12

___ 1 Thessalonians 1:6-8

II. *(Matching Alphabetical letter to the word)*

___ Character

___ Settle

___ Perfect

___ Spiritual living

A. "To restore, to mend, to repair."

B. "Devoting oneself to knowing Jesus Christ"

C. "Before God releases His vision He first deals with..."

D. "To consolidate or to lay a foundation..."

TRUE/FALSE

Indicate whether the statement is T (True) or F (False)

1. _____Spiritual living seeks to live an obedient life to Christ.

2. _____Spiritual living describes the purpose of my heart.

3. _____Spiritual living is looking out for number one.

4. _____Spiritual living is filled with pride and ego.

5. _____Spiritual living affects the posture of the heart.

6. _____God looks for faithfulness, character and integrity.

**See Appendix for Answers

GROUP DISCUSSION AND APPLICATION

Sharing – How did it go this week?

[Opening prayer inviting the Holy Spirit to guide our time together]

Walking through the lesson:
- Review together the lesson you worked on this week about Spirit Living.
- What spoke to you the most?
- What challenged you the most?
- Which of the four keys to Spirit-filled living spoke to you the most and why.
- What do you struggle with the most in your spiritual life?
- What is your present devotional life like? On a scale of 1 to 5 (1 low and 5 high) where would you put your devotional life?
- What does it mean to drink daily of God's Spirit and how can we do that?
- Why is spiritual living a choice we make daily? How are we learning to make that choice?
- What one truth do you feel God is calling you to from this lesson?

Oswald Chambers in his devotional book, *My Utmost for His Highest states,* "It is only when we get hungry spiritually that we receive the Holy Spirit" (p. 333).

"Common sense is a gift which God gave to human nature; but common sense is not the gift of His Son. Supernatural sense is the gift of His Son; never enthrone common sense" (Oswald Chambers, p. 222).

In contrasting the Mary Church and Martha Church -Terry Teykl, *The Presence Based Church* suggests, "Martha based church is centered around programs; we are busy in the kitchen cooking something up. It is consumer-based, what can we do to get more people? The Mary based church is centered around His presence; we are sitting before Him getting His direction and soaking in His presence; what must we do to get Him?"

Next lesson we will look at, *What is the Mark of a Fruitful Life?* Come ready to share!

Lesson 2

WHAT IS THE MARK OF A FRUITFUL LIFE?

I believe we all desire to live a fruitful life. There is not a one of us who doesn't want to hear those inviting words, "well done good and faithful servant; you have been faithful over a few things, I will make you ruler over many things. Enter into the joy of your Lord" (Matthew 25:23).

A fruitful life is filled with hope. "Christ in you, the hope of glory" (Colossians 1:27). "For there is hope for a tree, if it is cut down, that it will sprout again, and that its tender shoots will not cease though the root may grow old in the earth, and its stump may die in the ground, yet at the scent of water it will bud and bring forth branches like a plant" (Job 14:7-9).

† What causes the stump that is dead to live again?

_____

_____

† Why do we have hope and what is our hope based upon?

_____

_____

A fruitful life doesn't mean:
- Living the good life.
- Everything is just falling into place.
- The absence of trouble or challenges.

Objective | What then would be the mark of a fruitful life? I suggest the word *enduring*. The Bible defines enduring "as a hopeful fortitude that actively resists weariness and defeat. It also means to hold one's ground in conflict, to bear up against adversity, to stand firm, to wait calmly and courageously. It is not passive resignation to fate, but the active, energetic resistance to defeat that allows calm and brave endurance."

In order to live a fruitful life, we need to know what causes fruitfulness or barrenness in our lives. Turn now to Mark 4:13-20 and read this account of what it means to have a fruitful life.

LET'S LOOK AT FOUR KEYS TO SPIRITUAL LIVING

A. The path is *hard*. The seed of God's word falls by the wayside and the enemy comes and steals away the life changing, power producing word of God from our life (Mark 4:13-15). The indifference can be a lifestyle that one has chosen to live. It can also represent a season in ones life when we are not receptive or responsive to the word of God. God's word is unable to penetrate our heart and mind. As a result of that the enemy does what John records in his Gospel, "The thief does not come except to steal, and to kill and to destroy" (John 10:10).

† Describe what happens to God's word when it falls on hard ground.

_____

_____

† What does the hard ground represent?

_____

_____

_____

B. The soil that is *rocky*. We relate to God superficially, with no depth of faith in God's word. We hear the word and we receive it with joy. Yet when trouble, difficult times and challenges come crashing upon us we quickly lose our faith to endure (Mark 4:16-17). Rocky soil expects the worst and most of the time is not disappointed. The shallowness of hearing causes us to be knocked off course for when the winds of adversity come we have nothing to hold on to. That is when we need to be hearing what God is saying and what promise or word He is speaking that will get us through the adversity, so that we are not crushed like grapes beneath the weight of the pressure.

† Describe what the rocky soil is and how does it effect our life upon receiving God's word?

_____

_____

_____

_____

C. The soil that is *thorny*. This is the heart that is constantly distracted by the cares and worries of the world. The word of God is choked out, making one unfruitful (Mark 4: 18-19). The word *cares* is made up of two words, *to divide* and *the mind* meaning to have two minds and wavering between hope and fear. *Cares* denotes distractions, anxieties, burdens and worries. Peter in his Epistle instructs to "Cast all your cares upon Him, for He cares for you" (1 Peter 5:7).

† Describe what the thorny soil is and in what ways does it affect our life?

_____

_____

_____

D. The soil that is *good* is the enduring life of faith. This person receives: trusts and obeys God's word. That produces a crop of 30, 60 and 100 times what was sown (Mark 4:20).

† Describe the good soil and what would it take for you to have this kind of soil in your life?

_____

_____

_____

Responsive hearing of the word means:
- There is *openness* in our spirits to hear the truths and principles of God's word and seek to apply them to our lives. "Open my eyes, that I may see wondrous things from Your law" (Ps.119:18).
- There is a *teachable* spirit to receive all that the Lord intends for us to have and to receive. "Teach me Your way, O Lord, and lead me in a smooth path" (Ps. 27:11).
- There is a *readiness* in our spirits to cooperate with God's purpose and with what He is saying. Titus in his Epistle admonishes us to "Be ready for every good work" (3:1b).
- There is a *hunger* in our spirits to be fruitful in our walk and relationship to Jesus Christ. "Blessed are those who hunger and thirst for righteousness, for they shall be filled" (Matthew 5:6).

These are the qualities of living a fruitful life. Jesus said, "By this is My Father glorified, that you bear much fruit; so you will be My disciples...And that your fruit should remain" (John 15:8, 16).

† Describe why you think our Heavenly Father is glorified when our lives are bearing fruit. How do you think we can best bear fruit?

_____

_____

The Apostle Paul illustrates the enduring life that produces fruitfulness in these ways:

2 Timothy 4:6-8
- I have *fought* the good fight of faith.
- I have *finished* the race.
- I have *kept* the faith.

How then can we build an enduring life of faith that produces fruitfulness?

1. It is living an *obedient* life, because God blesses obedience. "Indeed we count them blessed who endure" (James 5:11).

    † Why do you feel that endurance can be a blessing?

_____

_____

2. It is enjoying the *promises* of God. "For you have need of endurance, so that after you have done the will of God, you may receive the promise" (Hebrews 10:36). "And so, after he had patiently endured, he obtained the promise" (Hebrews 6:15).

    † Why is endurance so difficult to cultivate in our lives?

    _____
    _____
    _____

3. It is keeping our *focus* on Christ while in the race. "Let us run with endurance the race that is set before us" (Hebrews 12:1). "He who endures to the end will be saved" (Matthew 24:13).

    † Why is it important to keep our focus upon Christ while running the race that is before us?

    _____
    _____

4. It is becoming *Christ-like*. "Looking unto Jesus, the Author and Finisher of our faith…who for the joy that was set before Him endured the cross…for consider Him who endured such hostility" (Hebrews 12:2-3).

† Why do you feel the race Jesus ran for Himself was one of joy? What difference does that make in how we run our race? Page 12

_____

_____

The Christian faith is not a passive faith but an active one. We are not only called to believe, but also to obey! True faith produces loving obedience. Holy desperation for God's presence creates an enduring faith that results in a fruitful life.

CLOSING PRAYER:

Lord, Jesus, we ask that You would cultivate our hearts by Your Holy Spirit so that we are able to hear with intention and to obey with a cheerful heart. We ask that we would so allow You to work in our hearts that produces the fruit that endures to the end. Lord, make us fruitful as a distinguishing mark of being Your disciple. Give us a willing spirit to obey You and experience Your presence in our lives in a profound way.

Journey in Discipleship

REFLECTION QUESTIONS

1. Describe one thing you learned from this lesson.

   _____

   _____

   _____

   _____

2. What challenged you the most about this lesson?

   _____

   _____

   _____

   _____

3. Do you have a greater understanding about living the Spirit-filled life and in what way will it affect your life?

   _____

   _____

   _____

   _____

What is the Mark of a Fruitful Life? | Study Guide

MATCHING

I. *(Match the number with the Scripture)*

1. "That produce 30, 60, 100 times what was sown."
2. "For you have need of endurance…"
3. "Christ in you, the hope of glory."
4. "And that your fruit should remain."
5. "Cast all your cares upon Him…"

___ 1 Peter 5:17

___ Colossians 1:27

___ John 15:8,16

___ Hebrews 10:36

___ Mark 4:20

II. *(Matching Alphabetical letter to the word)*

___ Teachable

___ Faith

___ Endurance

___ Rocky

___ Openness

A. "To bear up against adversity, to stand firm…"

B. "To hear the truths and principles of God's word…"

C. "With no depth of faith in God's word…"

D. "Receive all that the Lord intends…"

E. "I have fought the good fight of…"

True/False

Indicate whether the statement is T (True) or F (False)

1. _____ God does not want us to be fruitful as His disciples.

2. _____ God's intentions are that we hear and obey His word.

3. _____ We are to keep our focus on Christ.

4. _____ We are to fight the good fight of faith.

5. _____ We are to have a teachable spirit.

6. _____ A fruitful life is absent of obstacles and challenges.

***See Appendix For Answers*

What is the Mark of a Fruitful Life? | Study Guide

GROUP DISCUSSION AND APPLICATION

Sharing – How did it go this week?

[Opening prayer inviting the Holy Spirit to guide our time together]

Walking through the lesson:
- What spoke to you the most?
- Read Galatians 5:22-23. Which fruit of the Spirit are you asking God to work into your life?
- Which soil as described in Mark 13:20 characterize your life the best?
- What is the opposite of fruitfulness? What do you think causes barrenness?
- What one truth did you receive from this lesson?
- What is your prayer in becoming a more fruitful believer? Would you ask the Lord to fill you with His Spirit so that the fruit of the Spirit becomes even more alive and active in your life?

Fruitfulness is a result of being attached to the vine (Jesus). The more we cultivate this dynamic relationship to Jesus the more of His life flows through us and the greater fruitfulness we will experience (John 15:5).

Fruitfulness does not happen overnight, but

through constant diligence, patience and endurance we experience the transformation He makes in us that becomes evident to all. There are no shortcuts to bringing forth fruit that endures the test of time and lasts for eternity (John 15:16).

Fruitfulness does derive from straining more, doing more or trying harder, but from resting more and letting the Lord cause the increase (Mark 4:26-27).

The Bible admonishes us to "Be fruitful and multiply" (Genesis 1:22). Our life is to increase in fruitfulness through our spiritual progress and maturity in Christ. Yet our life is to have a larger context than ourselves. We are also to raise up spiritual offspring. That is, the seed of the life of God planted in us is to be planted into the lives of others. This is a mark of a fruitful life that glorifies God and causes His Kingdom to increase (2 Timothy 2:1-2).

Next lesson we will look at, *Fulfilling Our Spiritual Purpose*. Come ready to share!

Lesson 3

FULFILLING OUR PRIMARY PURPOSE

Objective | To discover that spiritual fulfillment addresses three main issues:

Why am I here? This speaks to the issue of significance.

Where am I going? This speaks to the issue of purpose and mission.

Finally, who am I? This speaks to the issue of our self-worth. The French physicist Blaise Pascal said, "God created man for a spiritual relationship with Himself."

† Why do you feel God created man with a vacuum that only He can fill?

_____

_____

Anna became a widow early on in her life and chose how she would spend the rest of her life – in the temple praying. I believe her prayers helped to usher in the King of Glory, Jesus, the Messiah, our Savior.

Anna represents the church. We too have the opportunity to usher in the King of glory as He would come and visit His people today.
- With those whose *focus* is clear.
- With those whose *determination* is marked with conviction.
- With those whose *calling* is contagious.
- With those whose *voice* sets the climate for spiritual renewal.

LET'S LOOK AT ANNA'S LIFE AND SEE HOW SHE ANSWERED THOSE PIVOTAL QUESTIONS

A. The first question she had to address was: *Why am I here?* That is, how is my life going to have meaning? Where will I find my sense of significance?

Anna, discovered that she was here to enjoy a relationship with the Lord of all the earth. We are here to live in fellowship with Jesus Christ. Many times we seek to find our significance in our work, our children's success, our possessions, our spouse, our good deeds, our degrees, our abilities, our investments, our appearance, or our accomplishments. She had to discover her *security* was in relating personally to the Lord.

Anna, in the midst of her tragedy, discovered her purpose for living and answered the question: Why am I here? It was to pray unceasing for the coming and visitation of the Lord. Zacharias, the father of John the Baptist, described the coming of Jesus, "Therefore the tender mercy of our God, with which the Dayspring (the dawning of the Messiah) from on high has visited us" (Luke 1:78-79).

For what purpose did Jesus come?
- To give *light* to those who sit in darkness.
- To give *life* to those who live in the shadow of death.
- To take *steps* toward a living relationship with Him, the Prince of peace.

Anna's life is best described in Psalm 26:8 "Lord, I have loved the habitation of Your house and the place where Your glory dwells." Anna's challenge was not to agonize over what she had missed, but to discover whom she would look upon and her eyes behold the Son of God.

† How can we use tragedy to discover God's will for our lives?

_____

_____

_____

_____

B. The second question Anna had to answer was: Where am I going? Jim Goll in his book, *Kneeling on the Promises* observes, "Anna must have been consumed with a burning passion sustained those many long years in what some would consider a state of inactivity. It takes prophetic vision to continue such a ministry long term."

Anna was a woman of the "secret place" in bringing the purposes of God to her generation. "He who dwells in the secret place of the Most High shall abide under the shadow of the Almighty." I will say to the Lord. "He is my refuge and my fortress; My God, in Him I will trust" (Psalm 91:1-2).

† In your own words describe what the "secret place" is and what we find there.

_____

_____

_____

_____

The Lord wants to deliver us from the *shadow of death* as describe by Zacharias to the *shadow of the Almighty* as described by the Psalmist.

Anna's security rested in knowing the Lord and that is why He would be her Source of strength and she would find in Him her Source of joy and fulfillment. This assurance sustained her through the quiet years when seemingly nothing was happening. We are simply called to be obedient to what the Lord has called us to be and to do and He will be our reward.

C. Finally, the third question Anna answered was: Who am I? She could have *depended* upon the wonderful heritage that was left to her. Her father was Asher, the eighth son of Jacob. His name means blessed or happy. As Jacob blessed each of his sons, he said of Asher, "He would bring forth a good harvest of pleasant things" (Deuteronomy 33:24-25). Asher's legacy would be long life and abundant energy.

Anna could have said, look at my heritage, my family tree and the blessing bestowed on my father by Jacob. Look at my spiritual heritage. Anna affirmed that, but said, I must have my own experience and relationship with the Lord.

From Anna's experience we see these truths:
1. She had such a relationship with the Lord that she could *recognize* the day of His visitation.
2. Her spirit *witnessed* that this was the Christ, the Son of God. She declared who He was and what He would come to do. "In that instant she gave thanks to the Lord, and spoke of Him (Jesus) to all those who looked for redemption in Jerusalem" (Luke 2:38).

† What do you think it felt like for Anna to see her prayer answered after all the days she had endured and all the hardship she had experienced?

_____

_____

_____

Anna calls the church to take on the *posture* of:
1. Knowing why the Church is here: To *pray* for the purposes of God to be accomplished in this present hour.
2. Knowing where we as the Church are going: To be a people who can know and recognize and embrace the *present* move of God so that we do not miss the day of our visitation.

3. Knowing who the Church is as described in Psalm 20:7: "Some trust in chariots, and some in horses; but we will *trust* in the name of the Lord our God."

† What would it take for us to have a visitation of the Lord? Would we recognize it when He comes? How can we prepare our hearts for such a visitation?

_____

_____

_____

Spiritual fulfillment is found first and foremost in a living, vital relationship to Jesus. As one church historian stated, *God has created man with a void that only He can fill.* Spiritual fulfillment is not in the doing, but in the being. Spiritual fulfillment is found in whose I am. That is, in being surrounded by the warm embrace of Jesus.

CLOSING PRAYER

Lord Jesus, help me to find my place of significance in You. Lord, let me find my greatest joy to be in Your presence and find in Your presence You fill those places where void and emptiness have dwelt. Lord, let me find in Your presence a place of shelter, safety and security. Lord, help me to find my spiritual fulfillment in You and in You alone. Amen!

REFLECTION QUESTIONS

1. Describe one thing you learned from this lesson.

   _____

   _____

   _____

   _____

2. What challenged you the most about this lesson?

   _____

   _____

   _____

   _____

3. Do you have a greater understanding about spiritual fulfillment and in what way will it affect your life?

   _____

   _____

   _____

   _____

Journey in Discipleship

MATCHING

I. *(Match the number with the Scripture)*

1. "But we will trust in the name of the Lord our God."
2. "He would bring forth a good harvest of pleasant things."
3. "The Dayspring from on high has visited us..."
4. "He is my refuge and my fortress; My God, in Him I will trust."
5. "Lord, I have loved the habitation of Your house..."

___ Psalm 91:1-2

___ Luke 1:78-79

___ John 15:8,16

___ Psalm 20:7

___ Deut. 33:24-25

II. *(Matching Alphabetical letter to the word)*

___ Voice

___ Significance

___ Relationship

___ Conviction

___ Prayer

A. "Our determination to be marked with.....?"

B. "God created man for a spiritual.....?"

C. "Why I am here addresses the issue of.....?"

D. "How will the purposes of God be accomplished in this hour?"

E. "What sets the climate for spiritual renewal?"

Fulfilling Our Primary Purpose | Study Guide

TRUE/FALSE

Indicate whether the statement is T (True) or F (False)

1. _____ God desires to have a spiritual relationship with us.

2. _____ Anna's focus was clear in praying for God's Kingdom to come.

3. _____ We are to trust in chariots and horses.

4. _____ My significance is found in what I do.

5. _____ We find our refuge and fortress in God.

6. _____ We are to pray for a visitation of God today.

7. _____ God created man with a void that only He can fill.

**See Appendix For Answers

GROUP DISCUSSION AND APPLICATION

Sharing – How did it go this week?

[Opening prayer inviting the Holy Spirit to guide our time together]

Walking through the lesson:
- What challenged you the most?
- What does spiritual fulfillment mean to you? How can we find spiritual fulfillment? What do you think keeps people from having spiritual fulfillment?
- How are some ways people seek to find spiritual fulfillment?
- Why is it important to know who we are in Christ? How does God see you? What would keep people from knowing and experiencing who they are in Christ?
- What does it mean – "spiritual significance?" What do you feel is most important: to know who we are in Christ or what can I do in the church?
- Do you feel that you are walking in spiritual fulfillment at this point in your life? If yes, why? If not, why?

Discovering our significance means we know that we are totally loved by God and that He accepts us unconditionally. That nothing we do or say will change His love for us. How much does God love us – as much as He loves His only Son, Jesus.

Our significance is not built on superficial things, like how much do we do for God, but on the reality of how much He has done for us. We cannot gain our significance by the approval of others, but on the fact that God knows us and His heart is totally ravished.

Understanding our significance of who we are in Christ is one of the most important truths we can incorporate into our life, because it determines why we are involved in ministry and who we are doing it for. Understanding our significance allows us to say "yes" and to say "no". We already stand approved before God. We don't have to win His approval – He really does like us!

Next lesson we will look at, *What's All This Talk About Spiritual Warfare?* Come ready to share!

Lesson 4

WHAT'S ALL THIS TALK ABOUT SPIRITUAL WARFARE?

Objective | Our freedom in Christ is the renouncing of the hidden things so that the light of Christ can shine in the dark places and through His light expose the darkness. Then we experience the liberty we have in Christ and learn to keep short accounts with God. "Stand fast therefore in the liberty by which Christ has made us free, and do not be entangled again with a yoke of bondage" (Galatians 5:1).

The Church at times finds it difficult to identify the enemy. The Bible states, "For we do not wrestle against flesh and blood, but against principalities, against powers, against the rulers of the darkness of this age, against spiritual hosts of wickedness in the heavenly places" (Ephesians 6:12).

† Describe in your own words what freedom in Christ is.

_____

_____

_____

† Describe in your own words what spiritual warfare is.

_____

_____

Some Scriptures that speak of our warfare:
† Paul writing to Timothy, "This charge I commit to you...according to the prophecies made concerning you, that by them you may wage the good warfare" (1 Timothy 1:18).
† "No one engaged in warfare entangles himself with the affairs of this life, that he may please him who enlisted him as a soldier" (2 Timothy 2:4).
† "For the weapons of our warfare are not carnal but mighty in God for pulling down strongholds" (2 Corinthians 10:4).

† Why are we involved in spiritual warfare?

_____

_____

_____

As believers sometimes are not sure which is going to win out - good or evil. We hope in the end good will win out. We as believers must understand we are not in a system called dualism which is defined as good warring against evil hoping that good will win out. A good example of this is "Star Wars." It is a battle between Luke Skywalker and Darth Vador as good fighting the forces of evil. Rather, for the believers the war was won at Calvary and Jesus won the victory.

Paul explains what Jesus did on the cross: "having disarmed principalities and powers, He made a public spectacle of them, triumphing over them..." (Colossians 2:15).

James, who is the brother of Jesus, describes in his epistle three ways we are to do spiritual warfare as believers in Christ Jesus.

A. "Therefore submit to God" (James 4:7a). "If you still remain in this land, then I will build you and not pull you down, and I will plant you and not pluck you up. I will relent concerning the disaster that I have brought upon you" (Jeremiah 42:10).

The word, *submit* means *to stand under*. It suggests obedience, submission and subjection.

† Why is it important to live our lives submitted to God? What does it mean to submit your life to God?

_____

_____

_____

As we submit ourselves to God:
- He *builds* us up. He encourages us. He gives us a foundation upon which to build.
- He *plants* us for the purpose of bringing forth fruitfulness.
- He makes it a place of *restoration* and not disaster.

B. "Resist the devil (the enemy, our adversary) and he will flee" (James 4:7b). Paul writes, "Therefore take up the whole armor of God, that you may be able to withstand (resist) in the evil day, and having done all, to stand" (Ephesians 6:13).

The word, *resist* means, *to cause to stand.* It suggests vigorously opposing, bravely resisting, standing face-to-face against the adversary, standing your ground.

† Identify and list each of the parts of the armor of God found in Ephesians 6:14-17.

_____

_____

_____

_____

_____

Peter writes, "Be sober (self-controlled), be vigilant (watchful); because your adversary the devil walks around like a roaring lion, seeking whom he may devour, resist him, steadfast in the faith..." (1 Peter 5:8-9a).

† How do we resist the enemy? How can we be vigilant against the enemy?

_____

_____

_____

_____

C. "Draw near to God and He will draw near to you" (James 4:8a). "...Pray for us to the Lord your God...that the Lord your God may show us the way in which we should walk and the thing we should do" (Jeremiah 42:2-3).

"But it is good for me to draw near to God..." (Psalm 73:28). "Let us draw near with a true heart in full assurance of faith..." (Hebrews 10:22).

† What is the purpose of drawing near to God as it relates to spiritual warfare? Describe in your own words what it means to bring every thought captive to the obedience of Christ?

_____

_____

_____

How are we to come to the Lord or to draw near to Him?

The Psalmist concludes coming to the Lord with a pure, clean heart. Before going into the temple the priests stopped at the laver to wash their hands. "Who may ascend into the hill of the Lord? Or who may stand in His holy place? He who has clean hands and a pure heart" (Psalm 24:3-4).

† How are we to come to the Lord or to draw near to Him? Why is this important in doing spiritual warfare?

_____

_____

_____

The Psalmist exhorts coming to the Lord with a singleness of mind and heart. "One thing I have desired of the Lord, that will I seek: That I may dwell in the house of the Lord all the days of my life, to behold the beauty of the Lord, and to inquire in His temple," *(*Psalm 27:4).

† What shall be the attitude of our heart and mind as we draw near to God?

_____

_____

_____

We have discovered that spiritual warfare means:
1. *Submitting* ourselves to the Lordship of Jesus Christ.
2. *Resisting* the devil, the enemy and our adversary who comes only to "steal, kill and to destroy"

(John 10:10). The enemy is like a roaring lion seeking whom he may devour (1 Peter 5:8-9a). "...For we are not ignorant of his schemes" (2 Corinthians 2:11).
3. *Drawing near* to God. "For the weapons of our warfare are not carnal but mighty in God for pulling down strongholds" (2 Corinthians 10:4).

Let's do as Jeremiah encouraged those who came to him to pray on their behalf. *To remain in the land.* That is, stay faithful where God has planted you. Trust the Lord to provide your every need so that you inherit the promise that God will:

- *Build* you up. He will strengthen you and abide in you.
- *Plant* you. He will make you fruitful where you are.
- *Bless* you and begin to turn things around and redeem what has been lost or stolen.

Spiritual fulfillment is found first and foremost in a living, vital relationship to Jesus. As one church historian stated, *God has created man with a void that only He can fill.* Spiritual fulfillment is not in the doing, but in the being. Spiritual fulfillment is found in whose I am. That is, in being surrounded by the warm embrace of Jesus.

CLOSING PRAYER

Lord, thank you for the victory Jesus won for me on the cross by defeating the enemy. Help me to fight the fight of faith and to stand my ground against the evil forces that would seek to undo me. Lord, I draw near to you, to obey your voice.

REFLECTION QUESTIONS

1. Describe one thing you learned from this lesson.

   _____

   _____

2. What challenged you the most about this lesson?

   _____

   _____

3. Do you have a greater understanding about spiritual warfare and spiritual freedom and in what way will it affect your life?

   _____

   _____

   _____

MATCHING

I. (Match the number with the Scripture)

1. "Resist him, steadfast in the faith..."
2. "But it is good to draw near to God..."
3. "The weapons of our warfare...are mighty..."
4. "...And having done all to stand..."
5. "Let us draw near with a true heart..."

____ **Hebrews 10:22**

____ **Ephesians 6:13**

____ **Psalm 73:28**

____ **1 Peter 5:8-9a**

____ **2 Corinthians 10:4**

II. (Matching Alphabetical letter to the word)

____ **Plant**

____ **Resistance**

____ **Dualism**

____ **Submit**

____ **Obedient**

A. What we are to be toward the voice of God.

B. Good and evil warring against one another.

C. To stand under and suggest obedience.

D. "To cause to stand and suggest brave..."

E. To make you fruitful where you are.

TRUE/FALSE

Indicate whether the statement is T (True) or F (False)

1. _____ It is useless to fight against the enemy.

2. _____ Jesus defeated the devil on the cross.

3. _____ The devil is like a lion seeking someone to devour.

4. _____ I cannot resist evil.

5. _____ We are not sure good or evil will win.

6. _____ We are to wage a good fight.

7. _____ I come before the Lord with a pure heart.

**See Appendix For Answers

GROUP DISCUSSION AND APPLICATION

Sharing – How did it go this week?

[Opening prayer inviting the Holy Spirit to guide our time together]

Walking through the lesson:
- What do you think spiritual freedom means? What is the opposite of freedom?
- What are some common areas of bondage that people experience? What do you think would keep someone from experiencing spiritual freedom? How do you think bondages can keep us from living the abundant Christian life?
- What are some ways in which we can resist the enemy? What does it mean to submit to God? Why have we had little or no instruction about spiritual warfare?
- How are some ways people seek to find spiritual fulfillment?
- What does it mean when our warfare is not through carnal means? How can strongholds develop in one's life?
- Why do you feel knowing God's word is so important in doing spiritual warfare? Why is

putting on the whole armor of God important to keep one's self spiritually alert when it comes to spiritual warfare?

Ed Silvoso defines a stronghold as a, "mind set impregnated with hopelessness that causes the believer to accept as unchangeable something that he/she knows is contrary to the will of God" *Possessing the Gates of the Enemy,* by Cindy Jacobs, p. 102.

Beth Moore in her book *Praying God's Word* defines a stronghold as "Anything that exalts itself in our minds, 'pretending' to be bigger or more powerful than our God. It steals much of our focus and causes us to feel overpowered. Controlled. Mastered. Whether the stronghold is on addiction, unforgiveness toward a person who has hurt us, or despair over a loss, it is something that consumes so much of our emotional and mental energy that abundant life is strangled..."

A divine stronghold is "A state of total surrender to the mind of Christ in which He is the Most High God, and everything bows to the knowledge and experience of His presence" Terry Teykl, *Divine Strongholds.*

STAYING FREE IN CHRIST

"So Christ has really set us free. Now make sure that you stay free, and don't get tied up again in slavery" (Galatians 5:1).

✝ *Put on the armor of God daily* (Ephesians 6:13-17).

- I put on the helmet of salvation. I have the mind of Christ.
- I put on the breastplate of righteousness. I have the righteousness of God in Christ Jesus.
- I put on the belt of truth. I put on Jesus, who is the Way, the Truth and the Life.
- I put on the shoes of the Gospel of peace.
- I take up the shield of faith to quench all the fiery darts of the enemy.
- I take up the sword of the Spirit, which is the Word of God that helps me to discern between what is of God and what is not of God.

✝ *Declare no weapon formed against you will be able to prosper.* "For the weapons of our warfare are not carnal but mighty in God for pulling down strongholds, casting down arguments and every high things that exalts itself against the knowledge of God, bringing every thought into captivity to the obedience of Christ" (2 Corinthians 10:4-5).

† *Declare your freedom in Christ.* "And you will know the truth, and the truth will set you free" (John 8:32). "So if the Son sets you free, you will indeed be free" (John 8:36).

† *Keep short accounts with God.* Stay current in your relationship with the Lord. "But if we are living in the light of God's presence, just as Christ is, then we have fellowship with each other, and the blood of Jesus, His Son, cleanses us from every sin" (1 John 1:7, also Psalm 139:23-24).

Read and pray through these passages of Scripture for the next 21 days.

1 Corinthians 13; Galatians 5:22-25; John 15:1-13; Ephesians 1:15-23, 3:14-21; Philippians 1:3-10.

**Next lesson we will look at, *When it Comes to Spiritual Direction – I'm Challenged!*
Come ready to share!**

Lesson 5

WHEN IT COMES TO SPIRITUAL DIRECTION- I'M CHALLENGED.

In Mark 8:22-26 Jesus entered the town of Bethsaida and was mobbed by a crowd asking Him to touch their friend that he might receive his sight. Jesus was moved by the prayers of the people to touch their friend.

Objective | How many of us have cried out for a new vision and allowed the Lord to lead us from an old vision to the new thing God is doing? Sometimes our familiar surroundings tend to blind us. Jesus led the blind man out of town to heal him. The first time He touched his eyes, vision came, but it was not clear. We want clear spiritual direction for our lives, even if we have to persist to receive God's vision for us and His people.

A. The blind man brought to Jesus realized he needed someone to lead him. "So He took the blind man by the hand and led him" (Mark 8:23). The Psalmist declares,

"Lead me in the way everlasting" (139:24).

Isaiah states how the Lord will lead His people. "I will bring the blind by a way they did not know; I will lead them in paths they have not known. I will make darkness light before them" (42:16). Jesus said, "...And He calls His own sheep by name and leads them out" (John 10:13).

Joshua said to the people of Israel as they went through the Jordan River into the Promised Land, *"You have not passed this way before"* (Joshua 3:4).

God is able to lead us only if we realize that we need His leadership. We need to be led by Him – we need spiritual direction.

† Why do we need spiritual vision? What keeps us from receiving spiritual vision?

_____

_____

_____

B. This blind man needed the hand of Jesus to lead him where he could not go by himself. "...And (Jesus) led him out of town" (Mark 8:23).

This speaks of four ingredients needed for Jesus to lead us:
- It speaks of our dependence upon the Lord.
- It will require that we trust Him.
- It will demand our surrendering to His leading.
- It demonstrates the necessity of childlike faith.

This picture of trust and dependence illustrates that our Lord will lead us into unfamiliar places so that He can touch us at our deepest need – which is to know Him even better.

C. This blind man was willing for the Lord to do whatever it took to receive his sight. "And when He had spit on his eyes and put His hands on Him, He asked him if he saw anything" (Mark 8: 23).

The only other time Jesus spat on someone is found in Mark 7:33 when He healed the deaf-mute. "And He took him aside from the multitude, put His fingers in his ears, and He spat and touched his tongue."

† Why do you think Jesus spat on this man's eyes? Why do you think Jesus asked if he saw anything?

_____

_____

_____

Spiritual vision comes as we allow the Lord to touch our spiritual eyes so that we might see things from His perspective. Let us ask the Lord for true spiritual vision.

D. This blind man was led by Jesus to a place where he realized he needed yet another touch. He needed a second touch. "Then He put His hands on is eyes again and made him look up. And he was restored and saw everything clearly" (Mark 8: 25).

† Why was Jesus' second touch so important? How do we need God's second, third, touch upon our lives?

_____

_____

_____

We gain from this verse these three truths:

- God desires to restore our vision.
- God delights in taking us by the hand and leading us where He wants to take us.
- God will deliver us from the familiar and the comfortable and takes us to a new place in Him, because He loves us too much to leave us as we are.

† In what ways do you need a second touch of Christ upon your life?

_____

_____

_____

Do you need a second touch? Do you need the Lord to give you clarity of vision?

CLOSING PRAYER

Lord Jesus, I need Your leadership in my life. I need to hear your voice saying, "This is the way, walk in it" (Isaiah 30:21). Lord, where I have lost my vision for my life, my calling, I ask that You would restore that vision. Lord Jesus, give me true spiritual vision that I may see what you are doing and blessing and begin doing that. Lord, take my hand and lead me in the truth that sets me free to follow you, to know you and to be empowered by Your Holy Spirit.

Reflection Questions

1. Describe one thing you learned from this lesson.

   _____

   _____

2. What challenged you the most about this lesson?

   _____

   _____

3. Do you have a greater understanding about spiritual direction and in what way will it affect your life?

   _____

   _____

   _____

MATCHING

I. (Match the number with the Scripture)

1. "You have not passed this way before."
2. "And He was restored and saw everyone clearly."
3. "Lead me in the way everlasting."
4. "I will make darkness light before them."
5. "He calls His sheep by name."

____ John 10:3

____ Joshua 3:4

____ Mark 8:25

____ Psalm 139:24

____ Isaiah 42:16

II. (Matching Alphabetical letter to the word)

____ Demonstrates

____ Receive

____ Dependence

____ Deliver

____ Realization

A. God is able to lead us if we realize that we need to be led.

B. God will take us from the familiar and comfortable.

C. Doing whatever it takes to get our sight.

D. Jesus leading us speaks of our _____ upon the Lord.

E. Jesus leading us shows childlike faith.

Journey in Discipleship

TRUE/FALSE

Indicate whether the statement is T (True) or F (False)

1. _____ God desires to restore our spiritual vision.

2. _____ God wants to stretch our faith beyond the comfortable.

3. _____ I cannot trust God to lead my life.

4. _____ God knows my name and He leads me.

5. _____ God takes us in ways we have never gone before.

6._____ Allowing God to lead us means surrendering to His leading.

7. _____ Following Jesus is like the blind leading the blind.

**See Appendix For Answers

GROUP DISCUSSION AND APPLICATION

Sharing – How did it go this week?

[Opening prayer inviting the Holy Spirit to guide our time together]

Walking through the lesson:
- Why was it important that Jesus takes the blind man by the hand and leads him? What did Isaiah mean when he recorded these words, "I will bring the blind by a way they did not know; ... I will make darkness light before them" (Isaiah 42:16) What does that mean in the life of a believer?
- What do you feel are the qualities necessary for us to be led by the Holy Spirit?
- Why do you feel it took a second touch of Jesus for this man to see clearly? What do you think may have prevented him from seeing clearly in the first place? Are there times in our own lives when we need a second touch of Jesus upon our lives? Why and when?
- What does this experience tell us about our need of spiritual vision, to see what the Lord is doing and for Him to direct our lives? How can we become more confident about God's leadership in our lives?

- In what area(s) of your life do you need God's touch, even His second, or third, touch? In what areas of your life do you need clarity of vision? How is God leading you from the familiar to the new thing He is doing?

Developing a God-given vision begins in prayer by asking the Father to open the eyes of our heart to see what He is doing, saying and blessing at that moment. Spiritual vision may be given in portions, little by little, until the pieces begin to make sense. The Bible states, "We prophesy in part...we know in part" (1 Corinthians 13:9, 12).

God's leadership in our lives is powerful, profound and problematic. It is powerful because we see the divine hand of God upon our lives and we are grateful. It is profound because we are overwhelmed by the love of God that He cares so much He takes us by the hand and leads us. It is problematic because it disrupts our comfort zone. We are misunderstood and labeled as fanatics, but be of good cheer, because there have been many who have gone before us in the same manner.

Next lesson we will look at, *Learning to Pray in the Power of the Spirit*. Come ready to share!

Lesson 6

LEARNING TO PRAY IN THE POWER OF THE SPIRIT.

Objective | To examine biblical truths and principles of Christian community, why Christian community is crucial in building relationships that assist us to grow and mature in Christ, finally, discover ways which Christian community can find authentic expression.

If someone asked you who has influenced you in your Christian formation? Who has served to point you toward growing in Christ? We probably could identify one, two, three or more people who have impacted our lives. I think of Mrs. Young, my Sunday school teacher.

The Lord has created us in such a way that we need to be connected to one another, to encourage one another in the faith. We need people who love us as we are and see what we can become in Christ. As Howard Snyder in his book *The Problem of Wineskins* observes, "The church is a covenant community...every church has to wrestle with the cost of discipleship as it relates to being a part of this community of Jesus Christ."

The Apostle Paul had that kind of relationship with Timothy, "To Timothy, a true son in the faith" (1Timothy 1:2). Paul recommends Timothy, "But you know his proven character, that as a son with his father he served with me in the gospel" (Philippians 2:22).

The Bible is clear about Christian community and the kind of relationship we are to have with those like-minded believers.
"You also, as living stones, are being built up as a spiritual house" (1 Peter 2:5). "From whom the whole body, joined and knit together by what every joint supplies" (Ephesians 4:16). "But if we walk in the light as He is in the light, we have fellowship with one another..." (1 John 1:7).

† What is the purpose of Christian fellowship? Why is it so important to the life and health of the church?

_____

_____

_____

LET'S EXAMINE FIVE INGREDIENTS NEEDED TO BUILD HEALTHY SPIRITUAL RELATIONSHIPS:

A. First of all, spiritual relationships are undergirded by prayer, "...As without ceasing I remember you in my prayers night and day" (2 Timothy 1:3). Paul writes to the church at Rome, "...That without ceasing I make mention of you always in my prayers" (Romans 1:9)

† What makes prayer so vital in building healthy spiritual relationships?

_____

_____

_____

To grow is a choice to make, to position ourselves with a heart of humility, desire and discipline to go beyond where we presently are. Peter writes, "But grow in the grace and knowledge of our Lord and Savior Jesus Christ" (2 Peter 3:18).

B. Second, spiritual relationships means we are free to be ourselves and express ourselves openly and honestly. "Greatly desiring to see you, being reminded of your tears, that I may be filled with joy" (2 Timothy 1:4).

Paul writes, "...for three years I did not cease to warn everyone night and day with tears" (Acts 20:13).

† When have you experienced authentic Christian fellowship where you could be yourself and be totally loved and accepted? What would it take for that to happen?

_____

_____

_____

In the Christian community we learn to laugh, cry and to experience the joy of the Lord.

C. Third, in spiritual relationships we share a spiritual heritage with those we care about. "When I call to remembrance the genuine faith that is in you, which dwelt first in your grandmother Lois and your mother Eunice, and I am persuaded is in you also" (2 Timothy 1:5).

We discover *three key elements* that influence and impact others with the transforming power of the Gospel of Jesus Christ:

- They *communicated* their faith.
- They modeled their *commitment* to Christ.
- They *created* an atmosphere where others could respond to Christ's love.

We too, can share these same qualities toward those we love and care about. The Christian community where we engage ourselves to grow in Christ-likeness, to become authentic witnesses to the transforming power of Jesus Christ, to be ambassadors of Christ as we take Jesus to all the people and to welcome others into God's family in the context of Christian community.

D. Fourth, spiritual relationships assist us in identifying God-given gifts. "Therefore I remind you to stir up the gift of God which is in you through the laying on of my hands" (2 Timothy 1:6). Paul writes, "This charge I commit to you, son Timothy, according to the prophecies previously made concerning you, that by them you may wage the good warfare" (1 Timothy 1:18). Paul exhorts, "Do not neglect the gift that is in you, which was given to you by prophecy with the laying on of the hands of the eldership" (1 Timothy 4:14).

† Why has God given gifts to believers? Have you identified your spiritual gift? Are you presently involved in a Christian fellowship that is helping you to discern your spiritual gift?

_____

_____

_____

E. Finally, spiritual relationships remind us what we have in Christ Jesus, "For God has not given us a spirit of fear, but of power and of love and of a sound mind" (2 Timothy 1:7).

The fruit of spiritual relationships is found in these truths:

- We are able to experience the *power* of Christ working in our lives.
- We are able to know and experience the *love* God has for us.
- We are able to *discern,* know and apply God's will and purpose to our lives, *"For we have the mind of Christ."*

Spiritual relationships mean we have something to *pass on* to someone else. What we have to pass on is *discovered in Christian community* called fellowship and is the reason we are here today. Because someone else *shared their faith* in Christ, the *seeds of the Gospel were sown into* our lives, *watered by the Holy Spirit,* and has brought forth God's fruitfulness into our lives.

Developing Christian community is not an option. It is what *sustained* the early church and caused it to impact entire cities, towns, tribes and nations. It *saturated* the places of business, community life, and the very atmosphere was impacted by its display of love, sharing and care. It is what *sparked* revival, renewal and restoration to that which had become lifeless, empty, irrelevant and visionless. It *stirred* passion within the hearts of people that discovered the transforming power of Jesus Christ and the empowerment of the Holy Spirit in the context of the Christian community.

Spiritual relationships do not happen by accident, but are *intentional* and allows us to build *authentic* relationships with others, before we spend eternity with them. It allows the *cultivation* of spiritual growth, maturity and the discovery and use of Spiritual gifts God has given to us. Finally, it provides a way of *infiltrating* the community around us with the Good News of Jesus Christ and touching the lives of others that makes an eternal difference.

† What would it take for you to be in relationship with a small group of people that meet on a regular basis for the purpose of fellowship, discipleship, evangelism and with the goal of multiplication?

_____

_____

_____

† What are we doing to cultivate Christian community and to build healthy spiritual lives?

_____

_____

_____

How would you answer these questions:
- Who is helping you to grow in Christlikeness?
- Who are you helping to grow in Christlikeness?
- Who is helping you to identify your spiritual gifts?
- Who are you helping to identify their spiritual gifts?
- What would it take for you to be in relationship with a small group of people that meet on a regular basis for the purpose of fellowship,

discipleship, evangelism and with the goal of multiplication?
- What are we doing to cultivate Christian community and to build healthy accountability?

REFLECTION QUESTIONS

1. Describe one thing you learned from this lesson.

   _____

   _____

2. What challenged you the most about this lesson?

   _____

   _____

3. Do you have a greater understanding about spiritual relationships and in what way will it affect your life?

   _____

   _____

   _____

Journey in Discipleship

MATCHING

I. *(Match the number with the Scripture)*

1. "Stir up the gift which is in you..."
2. "Do not neglect the gift that is in you..."
3. "...I make mention of you always in my prayer..."
4. "...Are being built up as a spiritual house..."
5. "...We have fellowship with one another..."
6. "...Grow in the grace and knowledge of our Lord..."

___ 1 Peter 2:5

___ 2 Peter 3:18

___ 2 Timothy 1:6

___ 1 John 1:7

___ 1 Timothy 4:14

___ Romans 1:9

II. *(Matching Alphabetical letter to the word)*

___ Relationships

___ Discipleship

___ Engage

___ Prayer

___ Gifts

A. "Every church has to wrestle with the cost of..."

B. "Spiritual relationships are undergirded by..."

C. "Spiritual relationships assist us in identifying God-given..."

D. "Christian community is crucial in building..."

E. "Christian community is where we _____ ourselves to grow."

TRUE/FALSE

Indicate whether the statement is T (True) or F (False)

1. _____ We are to discourage the use of Spiritual gifts.

2. _____ To grow is a choice we make.

3. _____ Building Spiritual relationships is intentional.

4. _____ The early church was sustained by programs.

5. _____ We are called to stay within the walls of the church.

**See Appendix For Answers

GROUP DISCUSSION AND APPLICATION

Sharing – How did it go this week?

[Opening prayer inviting the Holy Spirit to guide our time together]

Walking through the lesson:

- Who influenced you toward becoming a Christian? In what ways did they influence you? What difference is it making in your life today?
- Who are you influencing for Christ? Whose life is different because you took time to sow the things of God into their lives? In what ways did you do that?
- Do you feel that we as the church are doing a good job at building spiritual relationships? Can you think of 3 to 8 people you would like to form a spiritual relationship with? What do you think it would take for that to happen?
- What would be your greatest fear in developing a spiritual relationship with others? How do you think you could overcome that fear?
- Would you be willing to pray for 3 to 8 people with whom you could build a spiritual relationship? Would you want others to join with you in that prayer?

"It is my conviction that the fellowship of the Holy Spirit is most likely to be experienced when Christians meet together informally in small group fellowship," Howard Snyder, *The Problem of Wine Skins,* p. 98.

"Methodically speaking, the small group offers the best hope for the discovery and use of spiritual gifts and for renewal within the church," Howard Snyder, *The Problem of Wine Skins,* p. 98.

"The small group was a basic aspect of the Wesleyan Revival in England, with the proliferation of John Wesley's 'class meetings.' Today the church needs to rediscover what the early Christians found: That small group meetings are something essential to Christian experience and growth," *The Problem of Wine Skins,* p. 98.

Next lesson we will look at, *Jesus- the Ultimate Model of Spirit-filled Living*. Come ready to share!

Lesson 7

JESUS – THE ULTIMATE MODEL OF SPIRIT-FILLED LIVING

We look to Jesus – His life, His death and His resurrection. We see His healing touch upon the lame, the blind and the forsaken. We see His mercy and grace toward those who were in bondage to sin to set the captive free. We see the servant heart of Jesus in seeking out the lost, the lonely and the forgotten.

We look to Jesus – because we want to be like Him. For we too, desire to touch others with the love of Christ. We too desire to see the captive set free. We too desire to be dispensers of God's mercy and grace. We too desire to have the servant heart of Jesus – to hear someone say, *You're Christ to me.*

Objective | "Looking to Jesus" – not just as an example to try and follow, for Jesus modeled how to be about ministry and service. He modeled how to make disciples. Jesus knew when He said, *Follow Me,* He was saying, *Follow Me as I follow My Heavenly Father.* The only way to live like Jesus, follow Jesus, and model Jesus – is to have Jesus living His life through us.

From this passage in Hebrews 12 we discover at least three character qualities Jesus models for us to have in our life.

A. First of all, Jesus modeled the joyful life. "...Who for the joy that was set before Him endured the cross, despising the shame, and has set down at the right hand of the throne of God" (Hebrews 12:2).

James, the brother of Jesus writes "Count it all joy when you fall into various trials" (James 1:2). *"Count it all joy"* is a deliberate intelligent appraisal of the situation from God's perspective, seeing trials as a means of spiritual growth. We rejoice in the results of what God is doing in our lives and in the circumstances we are in.

Isaiah the Prophet speaks of what Christ will give to us, "...The oil of joy for mourning, the garment of praise for the spirit of heaviness" (Isaiah 61:3).

† Why was it important that Jesus joyfully endured the things He did? What difference would this make when we experience difficulties and trials?

_____

_____

_____

The joy Jesus gives is rooted in His divine nature:
- It is the *fruit* of the Spirit. "But the fruit of the Spirit is, love, joy, peace... (Galatians 5:22).
- It is the *promise* we receive as a result of our salvation. "Therefore with joy you will draw water from the well of salvation" (Isaiah 12:3).
- It is the result of an *abiding* relationship with Jesus. "These things I have spoken to you, that My joy may remain in you, and that your joy may be full" (John 15:11).

What is the joy level of your life? Do you need more joy? Are you presently living in the fullness of the joy of Christ in you?

_____

_____

_____

B. Second, Jesus modeled the enduring life. "...endured the cross, the shame...For consider Him who endured such hostility from sinners against Himself..." (Hebrews 12:3).

James again writes, "Knowing that the testing of your faith produces endurance" (James 1:3). He goes on to say, "Indeed, we count them blessed who endure..." (James 5:11). This conveys a positive steadfastness that bravely endures. The writer of Hebrews tells us what we are in need of, "For you have need of endurance, so that after you have done the will of God, you may receive the promise..." (Hebrews 10:36).

† What is the purpose of the trials and testing that comes into our lives? How can we respond to the trials and testing that come into our lives?

_____

_____

_____

So why do we need endurance?
- We need the *character* of Christ in us. The Apostle Paul writes, "My little children, for whom I labor in birth again until Christ is formed in you"

(Galatians 4:19). The word *formed* means a change in character, becoming conformed to the character of Christ.

- It speaks of the *faithfulness* to the task the Lord has given to us. Paul speaks of his faithfulness to the Lord's call upon his life. As he speaks before King Agrippa, he states, *"I was not disobedient to the heavenly vision"* (Acts 26:19). *"…Let us run with endurance the race that is set before us"* (Hebrews 12:1).
- It speaks of the need to *press* through the challenges and the adversity we face. "But we have this treasure in earthen vessels, that the excellence of the power may be of God and not of us. We are hard-pressed on every side yet not crushed; we are perplexed but not in despair; persecuted, but not forsaken; struck down, but not destroyed" (2 Corinthians 4:7-9).

† What is the purpose of endurance? In what area(s) is God calling you to endure, to have the fortitude where Christ is being formed in you?

_____

_____

_____

C. The last character quality we find in Jesus is an obedient life. Jesus demonstrated that the obedient life is the blessed life. He was obedient to His Heavenly Father so that we would not, "become weary and discouraged in your souls" (Hebrews 12:3). "...He became obedient to the point of death, even death on the cross" (Philippians 2:8). "And let us not grow weary while doing good, for in due season we shall reap if we do not lose heart" (Galatians 6:9).

We discover these truths:

1. Jesus is the example of not becoming weary, because He knew His *purpose* and *mission*.
2. Jesus is the example of not becoming weary, because He knew we would be *tempted* to give up before we would experience a breakthrough in our lives.
3. Jesus is the example of not growing weary, because He wanted to model the *sacrificial* life. "...But made Himself of no reputation, taking the form of a bond-servant, and coming in the likeness of men. And being found in appearance as a man. He humbled Himself and became obedient to the point of death, even the death of the cross" (Philippians 2:7-8).

† Why is knowing our purpose able to keep us going when we become weary, discouraged or tempted to give up? In a couple of sentences describe what your purpose is. How can the Christian community assist us in identifying our purpose?

_____

_____

_____

HERE IS OUR LORD'S PROMISE TO US:

"Come to Me all you who are weary and are heavy laden, and I will give you rest. Take my yoke upon you and learn from Me, for I am gentle and lowly in heart, and you will find rest for your souls. For my yoke is easy and My burden is light." (Matthew 11:28-30).

Journey in Discipleship

REFLECTION QUESTIONS

1. Describe one thing you learned from this lesson.

   _____
   _____

2. What challenged you the most about this lesson?

   _____
   _____

3. Do you have a greater understanding about Jesus: Our Spiritual Model and in what way will it affect your life?

   _____
   _____
   _____

Jesus – The Ultimate Model of Spirit-filled Living | Study Guide

MATCHING

I. *(Match the number with the Scripture)*

1. "Count it all joy when you fall into various trials."
2. "Let us not grow weary in doing good."
3. "For My yoke is easy and My burden is light."
4. "But the fruit of the Spirit is…"
5. "Who for the joy that was set before Him…"

____ **Hebrews 12:2**

____ **Galatians 5:22**

____ **James 1:2**

____ **Matthew 11:28-30**

____ **Galatians 6:9**

II. *(Matching Alphabetical letter to the word)*

____ **Salvation**

____ **Obedient**

____ **Purpose**

____ **Modeled**

____ **Faithfulness**

A. "Jesus showed us how to make disciples."

B. "Endurance speaks what we are to the task."

C. "The quality of life Jesus lived."

D. "Jesus is our example because He knew His…"

E. "The joy Jesus gives is rooted in our…"

True/False

Indicate whether the statement is T (True) or F (False)

1. _____ Jesus is our spiritual model.

2. _____ We are to complain when going through trials.

3. _____ When Christ is formed in us it changes our character.

4. _____ We can stand up under hard pressure because of Christ.

5. _____ We are to give into the temptations that come our way.

6. _____ We can come to Jesus and find rest for our souls.

**See Appendix For Answers

GROUP DISCUSSION AND APPLICATION

Sharing – How did it go this week?

[Opening prayer inviting the Holy Spirit to guide our time together]

Walking through the lesson:
- What challenged you the most about this lesson?
- Of all the ways Jesus modeled the spiritual walk with His Heavenly Father, what speaks to you the most?
- What do you think it means, "Looking to Jesus as the Author and Finisher of our faith?"
- What would it take to model your life after Jesus?
- In what ways do you want to model your spiritual life before others?
- What one way do you want to demonstrate the life of Jesus to others? What do you think it would take for that to happen?
- How did Jesus model discipleship? How did Jesus model leadership?
- What one thing are you seeking to apply to your life from this lesson?

We look to Jesus because:

"His of life, death and resurrection. We see His healing touch upon the lame, the blind and the forsaken. We see His mercy and grace toward those who were in bondage to sin to set the captive free. We see the servant heart of Jesus in seeking the lost, the lonely and the forgotten."

"We want to be like Him. For we too, desire to touch others with the Love of Christ. We too desire to see the captive set free. We too desire to be dispensers of God's mercy and grace. We too desire to have the servant heart of Jesus."

"He is not just as an example to try and follow; for Jesus modeled how to be about ministry and service. He modeled how to make disciples. Jesus knew when He said 'Follow Me,' He was saying, 'Follow Me as I follow My Heavenly Father.' The only way to live like Jesus, follow Jesus and model Jesus – is to have Jesus living His life through us."

Journey in Discipleship

NOTES

Journey in Discipleship

APPENDIX

ANSWER KEY

Lesson 1 | How Can We Live A Spirit-filled Life?

Matching		True/False
4	C	T
3	D	T
1	A	F
2	B	F
		T
		T

Lesson 2 | What is the Mark of a Fruitful Life?

Matching		True/False
5	D	F
3	E	T
4	A	T
2	C	T
1	B	T
		F

Lesson 3 | Fulfilling Our Primary Purpose

Matching		True/False
4	E	T
3	C	T
5	B	F
1	A	F
2	D	T
		T
		T

Lesson 4 | What's All This Talk about Spiritual Warfare?

Matching		True/False
4	E	T
3	C	T
5	B	F
1	A	F
2	D	T
		T
		T

Journey in Discipleship

Lesson 5 | When It Comes to Spiritual Direction – I'm Challenged.

Matching		True/False
5	E	F
4	D	T
2	B	T
1	C	F
3	A	F
		T
		T

Lesson 6 | Learning to Pray In the Power of the Spirit

Matching		True/False
4	D	F
6	A	T
1	E	T
5	B	F
2	C	F
3		

Lesson 7 | Jesus – the Ultimate Model Of Spirit-filled Living

Matching		True/False
5	E	T
4	C	F
1	D	T
3	A	T
2	B	F
		T

AUTHOR CONTACT

Should you have any questions or would like to contact the author you may do so at the information below:

Ray E. Petty Jr.
604 E. Elmwood St.
Jefferson City, TN 37760.
raypetty@hotmail.com.
(865) 748-6733